LEAVING LAS VEGAS

LEAVING LAS VEGAS
Mike Figgis

from the novel by John O'Brien

faber and faber
LONDON · BOSTON

First published in 1996
by Faber and Faber Limited
3 Queen Square London WC1N 3AU

Photoset by Parker Typesetting Service, Leicester
Printed in England by Clays Ltd, St Ives plc

Screenplay © Initial Productions SA, 1995

Afterword © Mike Figgis, 1996

Stills by Suzanne Hanover © Lumière Pictures Limited, 1995
Photo on p. 83 © Mike Figgis, 1995

Mike Figgis is hereby identified as author of this
work in accordance with Section 77 of the Copyright,
Designs and Patents Act 1988

A CIP record for this book
is available from the British Library
ISBN 0–571–17969–X

The author of the screenplay
wishes to thank Lila Cazès,
Producer of *Leaving Las Vegas*,
and Initial Productions SA,
for their courtesy in permitting
this publication.

2 4 6 8 10 9 7 5 3

CONTENTS

DISSOLVE TO:

I INT. SMART BAR IN BEVERLY HILLS. NIGHT

It is the kind of bar where the well-to-do folks of LA go to pick up – or be picked up. Lesser-known actors, agents and executives of all ages. Into this bar comes Ben.

Ben is in his thirties. He is wearing an Armani suit that could use a visit to the dry-cleaner's. He hasn't shaved in the last twenty-four hours (but neither has any of the actors in the bar). He is a good-looking man but is clearly in trouble of some kind. Although still in control of his faculties, it becomes clear in the following scene that he is much the worse for wear with drink. He looks around the room until he sees someone he recognizes and then walks over to a table where two couples are seated. The men are young execs, the girls, both blonde and busty, have very white teeth and smile all of the time. The camera follows Ben over to the table. One of the execs looks up as Ben gets close. He recognizes him but delays his recognition until the last moment in the hope that Ben is not looking at him.

BEN

Peter!

PETER

Ben . . . how are you, man?

They shake hands. Ben is not invited to take a seat and Peter waits for a while before being forced to introduce him to the table.

Ben Sanderson, Marc Nussbaum, Sheila, Debbie.

MARC

Nice to meet you. I think I spoke to you on the phone a couple of years ago. Weren't you both at MGM with Laddie?

BEN

That's right. Are you still at ICM?

MARC

No, I'm at Tri-Star now.

BEN

That's great. Say hello to Mike for me. That's a beautiful dress, Debbie, and those are fabulous earrings, Sheila.

There is an awkward silence. Ben does not make a move and is not invited to join them. The girls smile.

MARC

I gotta tell you, I'm a big fan of your writing. I loved *Bay of Pigs*.

BEN

Thanks a lot. I didn't actually write it, I just got the credit. I was fired.
(*to Peter*)
Can I talk to you for a moment?

Peter gets up and he and Ben walk to the door together. Peter speaks very quietly.

PETER

Listen, Ben, I can't help you any more. Do you understand?

BEN

This is the last time. Promise. I just need some cash tonight. I lost my credit cards. The money'll be on your desk first thing tomorrow morning, Scout's honour. How's the new one coming along? I hear you got Richard Gere.

The two men look at each other for a while. Peter's friends are looking at them, as are other people in the room. Peter takes out his wallet and extracts some notes.

PETER

This is all I have in cash. Please don't drink it here.

BEN

Yes, that's fine. I'll messenger it over to you tomorrow.

PETER

I don't want it. Ben . . . I think it would be best if you didn't contact me again.

And he turns and walks away, back to his table.
CUT TO BLACK:

TITLE: 'LAS VEGAS – 1.20A.M.'
FADE UP ON:

2 EXT. HELICOPTER SHOT. DAY

Las Vegas. A blaze of colour in the middle of a desert.

Credit sequence begins.
CUT TO:

3 INT. LOBBY OF EXPENSIVE HOTEL. NIGHT

A mixture of businessmen and gamblers creates a sense of activity and superficial excitement. Music wafts across the soundtrack, almost drowned by the dense texture of thousands of slot machines, creating an insane New Age symphony.

Credit sequence ends.

Into the lobby from the street comes Sera.

It's hard to tell how old Sera is – somewhere between twenty-five and thirty-five. She is a beautiful American girl. Her face has the freshness of a model in a Sears catalogue. She is dressed simply in a short black skirt and matching jacket. High heels complete the picture. Heads turn as she passes a group of businessmen and it's clear they find her very sexy. She acknowledges their glance with a half-smile and steps into the elevator. She could be a secretary, or a PA to one of the many execs here in Las Vegas at a convention. The body language is a bit different, though.

4 INT. PENTHOUSE SUITE OF HOTEL. NIGHT

A view of night-time Las Vegas through a window. Traffic up and down The Strip; bright, gaudy neon flashing and winking. We hear the sound of men laughing and the camera pulls focus and we see reflected in the glass . . .

. . . a group of people.

On the table are bowls of potato chips and dip and sandwiches. The TV is on at a sports channel and two boxers pound the shit out of each other.
   CUT TO:

5 INT. ELEVATOR. NIGHT

Sera looks at herself in the gold-tinted mirror in the elevator. She takes out a lipstick and freshens her lips. Some people get out and the elevator climbs higher. We see from the indicator that she has punched the Penthouse button. Camera moves in tighter and we see that she is nervous but concealing it well. The elevator stops, the doors open and she steps right into the Penthouse.

6 INT. PENTHOUSE. NIGHT

A bottle of Scotch is almost empty. The man talking is Yuri. He is Russian, in his early forties, a little overweight, a big man wearing a blue silk suit. His thick black hair is greased and combed back. He wears a lot of jewellery, all gold. Rings, a bracelet and a Rolex. Two men in business suits and a weird stoned woman in her late thirties listen to him.

YURI

. . . but please, my friends, call me Yuri. It is my American name . . . I picked it myself.

The three people laugh. There is a hint of contempt in the way that they speak to Yuri.

FIRST BUSINESSMAN

Where are you from, Yuri? I mean, you sure don't talk like you're from this neck of the woods.

Yuri smiles at them

YURI
(*silky voice*)

No . . . you are right, my friend. How very observant you are. I am from Latvia.

WEIRD WOMAN

Tough place.

YURI

Yes, I hear this too. But I am not a tough man. I am a simple man who is here to learn from my new American friends.

The door opens and Sera comes in. Everyone stares at her.

WEIRD WOMAN
(*turned on*)

Is this your friend, Yuri?

YURI

Ah, yes . . . Sera.

The Second Businessman takes out a manila envelope from his inside pocket.

Sera is my gift to you, my friends from New York City. You may do with her as you wish in this beautiful room, which is also my gift for the night to my friends. You will find her a very willing girl, for all of you . . . just as we arranged.

Yuri smiles again as the Second Businessman hands him the envelope. The rest of them just stare at Sera, aroused by the idea of her.

SECOND BUSINESSMAN

Of course, Yuri. I think you'll find this just as we discussed.

Yuri gets up.

YURI

So, my friends . . . I have other business to attend. Enjoy.

He heads for the door, passing Sera. She holds his arm as he passes.

SERA
(*whispering*)

Yuri . . . please! Can I talk to you for a moment.

Still smiling, he takes Sera's arm and leads her into the bedroom.

YURI

My friends . . . excuse us for just one moment.

7 INT. BEDROOM. NIGHT

Mirrors reflect mirrors.

SERA

I don't want this. Yuri, please. I really don't want this. You know I don't like to do groups.

YURI
(*playful*)

I want this, Sera. I need this!

SERA

Please, Yuri.

He holds out his arms. Sera goes to him. He hugs her with one arm. He pulls up her skirt so that her panties are exposed.

YURI
(*seductive*)

These are pretty.

Sera watches in the mirror as he pulls her panties to reveal her

6

buttocks. He strokes her there gently with his other hand. We see that there are two fine scars there. He speaks gently, like a father to a daughter.

Is this how you would repay me for coming all this way to find you again? Driving through the desert to protect my little Sera.
CUT TO:

FLASHBACK — SILENT — GRAINY BLACK AND WHITE

8 INT. ROOM. NIGHT

Yuri and Sera – different time, different place. Sera looking frightened, backing away from Yuri, who pulls a switchblade from his jacket and opens it.
CUT BACK TO:

9 INT. PENTHOUSE. NIGHT

Yuri enters from the bedroom. The weird woman is doing a line of coke.

> YURI
> (*cheerful*)

Sera wanted me to ask if she might undress at once for you. She has a very beautiful undergarment which she would like you to see.
ANGLE ON BEDROOM DOOR

Sera comes into the room. She smiles and begins unbuttoning her jacket.

She takes it off and drops it on the floor, and then unzips her skirt and steps out of it. Sera is now in control and playing the room. In the background. Yuri leaves the room.

> WEIRD WOMAN
> (*strange voice*)

Come here.

Sera walks over and something strange takes place between them.
CUT TO:

7

10 INT. BEN'S BAR. LA. MORNING

The bar is dark but through a small window we see that it is a very bright sunny day outside. The bartender reads the Los Angeles Times. *The bar surface is red vinyl. There are five customers, all single men. One of them is Ben and he is sitting at the bar watching TV. A game show is in progress and the TV sound is loud. Ben finishes his drink and grimaces before indicating to the barman that he'd like a repeat. Barman pours him a whiskey – Cranberry – and the camera moves in closer to Ben, ending up in a close-up. Ben takes a big hit from the drink and concentrates on the TV. We hear from the TV sound that it is a word game with a big prize. Ben smiles to himself.*

BEN'S POV OF TV

The talk show hostess, an American TV beauty, is showing the audience the prizes available in today's game show.

ANGLE ON BEN

As he finishes that drink and asks for another. The camera moves in close on his eyes.

BEN'S POV OF TV

She turns from the prizes and looks straight into the TV camera, which

*starts zooming into her. At first, what she is saying makes complete
sense, but then things change . . .*

HOSTESS
(smoky, sexy voice)

Just look at this studio, Ben, filled with glamorous merchandise,
including an extra special prize chosen just for you! A big, bad,
BMW motorcycle, complete with saddle bags stuffed with
thousands of US dollars.

There are 'oohs' from the audience.

So, Ben,

(tosses her hair)

let's find a bar, get drunk and go for a ride.

The studio lights dim.

Then we can get a suite somewhere and order up a case of
champagne while we fuck ourselves silly.

Close-up on males in audience doing the grunt.

This is it, just for you, Ben.

She unbuttons her top, licks her fingers and makes her nipples hard.

Because you've been so patient, and because I want to fuck you,
take care of you, and because there's nothing else in the world
worth doing.

Section of the audience clapping – some women dabbing their eyes.

Tell you what, Ben, let's go to Vegas. The bars stay open twenty-
four hours night and day. Just you, just me, Ben, think about it, all
right?

ANGLE ON BEN

Lost in this fantasy.

BEN

I'll think about it.

*He looks back at the screen, but the show has returned to what is
known as 'normal'. He finishes his drink and then an attack of
nausea hits him. He takes a deep breath and rolls his neck and his*

9

head. The barman puts down a fresh drink. Ben looks at his own hands . . . which are steady.

> **BARMAN**
>
> You should go on that show.
>
> CUT TO:

11 INT. SMART BUSINESS SPACE. MORNING

Ben sitting at a desk with a phone wedged on his ear, a cup of black coffee on the desk. The walls are covered with framed film posters and one complete wall has shelves jammed with scripts. He nods from time to time and sometimes says 'yes' or 'OK', but it becomes clear that there is no one on the other end. He drinks from the coffee cup. A woman comes up to his desk, a business colleague. She puts a wad of messages down on the desk.

> **BEN**
>
> Yeah, but what's the back end like? By the time we're through with P and A, the above-the-line is going to take it to about fifteen and with something like this . . . I don't know if Disney will go for it . . . can I call you back on this? OK . . . chow for now.
>
> *(to the woman)*
>
> Good morning.

> **WOMAN**
> *(cautious)*
>
> Ben . . . Mr Simpson was looking for you. I said that you had a doctor's appointment. He said for you to go in as soon as . . . are you OK?

> **BEN**
> *(pulling himself together)*
>
> I'm fantastic, but I gotta go out now . . . very important meeting, could make a coupla million for the company.

Ben gets up and as he passes her he grabs her and dances a few steps. It is clear that she likes Ben, but when his face gets close to hers she smells the alcohol on his breath and she turns away. Ben stops dancing and smiles sadly.

10

WOMAN
(*tender*)

Ben?

BEN

What?

WOMAN

You should go now.

She leaves the room and Ben goes through some routine at the desk.
He opens a drawer of a filing cabinet and puts in his whole arm,
looking for something at the very back. He pulls out a small vodka
bottle and opens it and then pours the contents into his coffee cup.
With cup in hand he leaves the room.
CUT TO:

12 INT. SMART OFFICE. DAY

Ben is sitting opposite his boss, Mr Simpson, who is very upset. He
hands Ben an envelope. Ben opens it and pulls out a cheque. He looks
at the amount.

BEN
(*genuinely moved*)

This is too generous, Peter.

SIMPSON
(*close to tears*)

Well . . . we liked having you around, Ben, but you know how it
is.

BEN
(*ashamed*)

Sure thing . . . and I'm sorry.

Ben takes a swig from his coffee cup.

SIMPSON
(*trying to cheer things along*)

Well . . . what are you going to do now?

BEN

I thought I might move out to Las Vegas.

11

Simpson looks puzzled.

The bars never close.

CUT TO:

13 INT. BEN'S BMW. DAY

Ben drives through Beverly Hills. He pours the contents of a small bottle of vodka into an empty Coke can, puts the empty bottle under the seat and then drinks from the can.

He slips a tape into the player and we hear 'Lonely Teardrops', by Michael McDonald, one of Ben's favorite songs. At a traffic light a cop on a bike pulls up next to him and Ben takes a pull from the Coke can and smiles, mouths the word 'hot'. The cop nods back at him, the light changes and they both pull away.

CUT TO:

14 EXT. SANTA MONICA STREET. DAY

Ben carries a brown paper bag which clinks. Camera follows him as he walks down the street. He looks at . . .

BEN'S POV

A girl walking ahead of him in the same direction. She is walking her dog. She is attractive from behind. We hear Ben's thoughts.

BEN
(*voice-over*)

Beautiful. Not just the shape, which is nice, but the whole walk, the feeling, the movement. This girl is pleased with herself. Maybe this is the only art I can appreciate . . . I don't know if this is good or bad, but right now she is really beautiful. When I was a boy it would have been really important that she have a very pretty face, to go with this body, I mean. I still would like to see her face, but her beauty is not dependent on her face.

The dog gets interested in something on the sidewalk and she bends down to pull at its collar.

I wonder what kind of panties she's wearing. Shit, that's too specific, but . . . on the other hand, you can never be too specific . . . but then, the infinitesimal must be, by definition, as infinite as the infinite.

Suddenly the girl stops. Ben catches up with her and cannot resist looking into her face.

> (*voice-over*)

God, she's so young.

The girl sees Ben and smiles an innocent smile.

> GIRL

Hi!

> BEN

Hi . . .
CUT TO:

15 EXT. BEN'S HOUSE IN SANTA MONICA. DAY

Ben walks up to his house still carrying the paper bag. A young boy of about thirteen years of age is fixing a beat-up bike. Ben greets him.

> BEN

Hey, Brad . . . how's it going?

> BRAD

Hey, Ben. There were a couple of guys looking for you.

> BEN

What did they look like?

> BRAD

Suits. I didn't tell them anything. You know anything about gears?

Ben takes a look. The gear mechanism is all bent out of shape. He bends down to have a look. It is clear from the way he deals with this mechanical problem that he is good with his hands. He doesn't try to force anything but he moves the chain and the gear mechanism to get to the problem.

> BEN

How'd this happen?

> BRAD

I was going real fast down on the beach and something slipped and everything got all jammed up.

BEN

The news is not good, kid. This bit here . . . see there . . . it's broken. You need a new one.

BRAD
(*upset*)

How much, do you think?

BEN

I don't know. I'll find out though.

Ben gets up, picks up his bottles and heads for his house. He looks back and Brad is sitting still by the bike, looking totally dejected. This really seems to upset Ben.
CUT TO:

16 INT. BEN'S HOUSE. AFTERNOON

Ben is naked and the shower can be heard in the background. The house is austere, only the minimum of furnishing. He pours a large tumbler of vodka and takes a gulp, then tops up the glass. He turns on the stereo, selects a record – Miles Davis, Kind of Blue *– and puts it on the turntable. He turns on the cassette recorder and inserts a new blank tape. He puts the machine into the record mode. He kneels down next to the deck and with complete precision puts the needle on the second track without any problem. The music starts and continues through the next sequence.*

17 INT. SHOWER. DAY

Ben in the shower with the glass in his hand.

18 INT. BATHROOM. DAY

Ben shaving with the glass in his hand. He does the area around his mouth first so that he can drink while he does the rest

19 INT. LIVING SPACE. DAY

Showered and shaved and wearing a smart dark suit, Ben looks handsome and normal. He selects another record and again sets up the cassette machine to record. He turns the stereo up full and dances by

himself while watching MTV silent. He tries a turn which is a bit
ambitious and loses his balance. In slow motion we see him fall. Ben lies
still on the floor. He smiles to himself and decides to stay there for a
while . . .

FADE OUT:

FADE IN:

20 INT. SERA'S BEDROOM. LAS VEGAS. DAY

Sera wakes up in bed next to Yuri. (The camera is high above the bed
looking down.) She is completely drenched in sweat. A thin shaft of light
comes from the crack in the drapes and falls across their bodies. Other
than that, the room is in darkness. To get out of bed she would have to
climb over him. She lies still. Yuri speaks without opening his eyes . . .

YURI

I missed you, Sera. You have been lonely?

Sera blinks and turns her head towards him.

SERA

I'm older now, Yuri.

He puts his hand between her legs, over the sheets and grasps her
there.

YURI

You have been lonely?

SERA
(tensing a little)

I've been all right.

YURI

I will keep you safe. We are both older.

He climbs on to her and mounts her. Familiarity.

You have been lonely?

SERA
(flat voice)

I am lonely, Yuri.

15

He begins thrusting into her.

> YURI

Yes . . . so am I.

Camera moves slowly into a tight portrait of Sera.

> SERA
> *(voice-over)*

I had a new dress . . . we were at the fair, Daddy bought me an ice-cream and I spilt it on my dress . . .

CUT TO:

21 INT. DOCTOR'S OFFICE. DAY

Sera is sitting on a sofa talking to an unseen person. (Although it is not entirely clear when this is taking place, the sense of it is that we are in the present, i.e. all the events in the film are in the past tense.)

> SERA

. . . Mom was with Helen, and Dad looked around first to see if she was watching and then he scraped it all off and threw it on to the grass and then he kissed me and hugged me and told me it was all right . . .

22 INT. SERA'S KITCHEN. LATER THAT DAY

Yuri is tucking into a hearty breakfast. Sera plays with her food.

> YURI
> *(planning his day)*

This is such a small apartment, Sera. I cannot stay here. We will find a big apartment. You know how much money I can bring you. I belong in . . .

> *(laughs)*

. . . wealth and luxury.

He suddenly looks up from his food and smiles at her.

Why did you run away from me in Los Angeles?

Sera says nothing.

Because you are sly. Mmm? You knew all along that there was more money in Las Vegas. Didn't you?

Sera nervously plays with her food.

You have nothing to fear from me. You know why? Because we belong together, Sera. Don't we?

Sera forces a smile.

SERA
(quietly)

Yes.

QUICK CUT TO:

FLASHBACK:

23 INT. ROOM. NIGHT

Grainy black-and-white image. Sera on a bed, pinned down by Yuri, who has a knife.

CUT BACK TO:

24 INT. SERA'S HOUSE. DAY

YURI

I'm pleased with you, Sera . . . how you have moved up in the world. I showed you a glamorous world when I took you off the streets . . .

(shaking his head)

and how you repay me.

SERA

Where have you been staying?

YURI

With an an old friend.

He drops his fork.

But that is none of your affair. You will call this morning and book me into a hotel suite where I will make new contacts for us.

The mood has changed and Sera does her best to move out of these dangerous waters.

SERA

You'll need some money, then.

Yuri nods. Sera rises, goes to a kitchen drawers and finds money.

YURI
(*becoming angry*)

It is, after all, Sera, my money.

SERA
(*calmly*)

Yes, of course. How much do you need?

YURI
(*shaking his head*)

All of it. I need to buy many things . . . all of it!

Yuri is very angry and as Sera hands him the money, he hits her, hard, knocking her back into the refrigerator. His ring cuts her cheek.

(*shouting*)

Don't look at me like that.

And then his anger goes and he becomes quite tender with her. He takes her face in his hands to look at the cut.

It's not so bad. It is nothing.
(*whispers*)

I need money, Sera. I need it fast. You must go on the street tonight. For me.

He sits down with shaking hands. He suddenly seems more vulnerable than she is. He goes to the window and looks out, left and then right, as if he expects to see something.

I need money fast, Sera. I want you back on the street. Tonight.

FADE OUT:

FADE IN SLOWLY – SOUND FIRST:

25 INT. BEN'S HOUSE. NIGHT

Ben opens his eyes. The only light comes from the TV. The Miles Davis record has got caught on a scratch and is repeating the same phrase over and over again. He looks at his gold Rolex and then fingers the wedding band on his finger.

CUT TO:

26 INT. BEN'S BAR. LA. NIGHT

Ben is sitting at the bar. He drinks a large glass of something very quickly and then immediately orders another.

He drinks this a little slower but still way too quick, finishes it and then orders another. He looks around the bar and sees a woman sitting by herself, thirtyish, pretty and receptive. She looks and sees Ben, and he smiles at her. She smiles right back. Ben talks across the bar.

> BEN
> (*charming*)

Good evening.

> PRETTY WOMAN
> (*pleased*)

Hi.

> BEN

I'm Benjamin . . . Ben.

> PRETTY WOMAN

I'm Teri.

Ben walks over to where she is.

She is pleased that this good-looking man has come over to make a play. She makes a noise with her straw to indicate that her glass is empty.

> BEN

I'll get you another one . . . and me too. Mind if I join you?

She watches him walk to the bar.

He gets the drinks and walks back to her. He sets the drinks down on the table and sits down. As he does so, his face gets close to hers and she smells the booze on him.

> PRETTY WOMAN

Wow . . . been drinking all day?

But of course.

She looks at him, a disappointed expression on her face. She is no longer interested in being seduced by this man and this much is clear to Ben.

Why don't we finish these and go to my apartment on the beach?

She doesn't respond.

We can watch a movie and I'll mix you up a gooey blender drink.

Ben winces at his own words. He shakes his head.

PRETTY WOMAN
I have to get up pretty early tomorrow. I'll just finish this and go. Thanks anyway.

They drink in silence for a while. Ben takes a deep breath.

BEN
(*pathetic*)
I really wish that you'd come home with me. You're so cute and I'm really good in bed . . . believe me . . . you smell good too . . .

He stops and frowns as he stares into his empty glass.

No, OK.

Ben tries to stand and has to pull himself up by holding the bar. It's a strange thing with drunks like Ben . . . when they're up they have balance and timing, but when they're down it all falls apart. She starts to speak but then doesn't. A look of great sadness comes over her.

PRETTY WOMAN
I have to go now. Thanks anyway.

She stands to go.

Maybe you shouldn't drink so much.

She walks to the door and Ben turns to the bar, watched by the Barman, who is a little concerned.

BEN
(*to himself*)
Maybe I shouldn't breathe so much, Teri. Ha . . . ha.

BARMAN
(*severe voice*)
Time to go, buddy . . . We're closing up.

Ben gets out his wallet but his hands are shaking so much that he cannot extract any bills. He is very embarrassed and tries again, but to no avail.

BEN
Would you . . .?

The Barman shakes his head in disgust as he goes into the wallet and takes some money.
CUT TO:

27 EXT. LA STREETS. NIGHT

Ben is cruising in his car, listening to music on his stereo.
CUT TO:

28 INT. STRIP CLUB. NIGHT

Ben comes into the club and sits down next to the stage, where a dancer is doing her thing accompanied by a live blues trio. A swimsuited waitress comes to the table.

WAITRESS
There's a one-drink minimum per show, I hope you saw the sign when you came in. Anyway, they're supposed to tell you.

BEN
Yes, I heard, and it's not a problem.

WAITRESS
What do you want?

BEN
What are my choices?

WAITRESS

Everything's ten dollars, and there's no alcohol.

BEN

No alcohol?

WAITRESS

No alcohol. You gotta get something else. Everything's ten dollars. What do you want?

BEN

What do you think I should get?

WAITRESS

Non-alcoholic malt beverage?

BEN

. . . Noooo.

WAITRESS

Orange soda?

BEN

No.

WAITRESS

Coffee?

BEN

No.

WAITRESS

Sparkling apple cider?

BEN

No.

WAITRESS

Water?

BEN

Water?

WAITRESS

One drink minimum per show. Everything's ten dollars. Now . . . tell me what you want or I'll eighty-six you.

BEN
(decides)

Water.

> *She writes down W.A.T.E.R. and walks away. Ben calls her back.*

Just how much would it cost for you to eighty-six me?

ANGLE ON THE STAGE

> *A tough black girl dances in a world of her own, impervious to the men who stare at her. The trio grinds out a dirty blues. A man opposite Ben places a dollar bill on the stage and as the dancer squats down to pick it up he stares between her legs and winks. The Waitress puts down a styrofoam cup and a bottle of water in front of Ben but refuses to look at him.*

WAITRESS
(hostile)

Three-fifty.

> *Ben puts down a hundred on to her tray.*

BEN
(polite)

Could I have fives please? Keep one for yourself.

> *This throws the Waitress for a loop.*

CUT TO:

29 INT. BATHROOM OF STRIP CLUB. NIGHT

Ben drinks all of a fifth of bourbon. Other guys come and go, pissing against the urinal.

Ben offers one of the guys a drink, the pianist from the trio. He takes a shot.

CUT TO:

30 INT. STRIP CLUB. NIGHT

Ben sits next to another man watching the show. On stage a tall blonde dances with her own reflection in a mirror. Ben turns to his neighbour.

BEN

To me there is nothing more beautiful than the relationship between the reflection of a woman and the woman who has created it.

NEIGHBOUR
(completely uninterested)

No shit!

30A EXT. LA STREETS. NIGHT

Ben drives in his car.

  CUT TO:

31 EXT. SUNSET BOULEVARD. LATER THAT NIGHT

Ben is cruising in his car, listening to 'Lonely Teardrops' again. He's looking for a prostitute. He sees a girl, but when he slows down she ducks into a doorway.

He looks in his rear-view mirror and sees a cop car coming up fast. Ben panics for a second. There is a bottle between his legs. The cop car draws level and cruises alongside him for a while, but then puts its lights and siren on and speeds off, doing a U-turn.

Ben continues and then sees an Hispanic girl and stops. He winds down the window. He is by now almost incoherent.

BEN

Good evening.

32 EXT. KERBSIDE. NIGHT

The girl looks up and down the street and then walks over to the car and bends down to the window.

HISPANIC GIRL

You wanna date? You wanna date me?

The girl's eyes shift constantly from Ben to the street and then back again.

BEN
(cut to the chase)

I'll give you a hundred dollars for a straight forty-five minutes. You get the room.

Ben shows her the money.

HISPANIC GIRL
(trying to take him)

The room is twenty. You pay for it.

Ben laughs.

BEN

OK . . . but only because I think that the concept of surrender fits in with the big picture right now. How about over there?

He gives her a twenty and indicates a motel across the street. She sets off and he gets out of the car. As he does, a wave of nausea hits him. He shakes his head violently and then lurches across the street, causing two cars to hit their brakes. The camera follows him into the dark parking lot of the motel, where the Hispanic girl is waiting.

(slurring badly)

I canrember . . . if mywifeleffme . . . or Ileff her . . . bufuckittanyway . . .

The girl laughs at Ben and says something in Spanish.

Slowly the picture gets darker, until all that can be seen is the headlights from the passing cars on Sunset . . . and then . . .
CUT TO:

33 INT. BEN'S HOUSE. DAWN

Ben wakes up on the kitchen floor. The fridge door is open and its light is what lights Ben. Inside the fridge are one green pepper and four bottles of vodka. Without too much effort Ben feels for his wallet and sees that it is still there, as are his car keys. He closes the fridge door and in the grey light from the window he lies still. The first birds start singing. (The birdsong continues through the following sequence, which does not have sync sound.)
CUT TO:

FLASHBACK

34 EXT. SUNSET BOULEVARD MOTEL. PARKING-LOT DUMPSTERS. NIGHT

At the rear of the motel. Next to some garbage hoppers, the Hispanic girl hugging him and kissing his neck. He tries to kiss her on the mouth, but she turns her face away.
CUT TO:

35 INT. BEN'S HOUSE. DAWN

Ben lying on the floor, thinking.
CUT TO:

FLASHBACK

36 EXT. SUNSET BOULEVARD MOTEL. PARKING-LOT DUMPSTERS. NIGHT

The Hispanic girl kneeling before him, unzipping his trousers. Through a gap in the fence, we see traffic going up and down Sunset.
CUT TO:

37 INT. BEN'S HOUSE. DAWN

Ben lying on the floor, thinking . . .
    CUT TO:

FLASHBACK

38 EXT. SUNSET BOULEVARD MOTEL. PARKING-LOT DUMPSTERS. NIGHT

The girl takes his hand and kisses it. She begins sucking the fingers, taking the whole hand into her mouth.
    CUT TO:

39 INT. BEN'S HOUSE. DAWN

Ben suddenly sits up and looks at his hand. His wedding ring has gone. He thinks about this for a long while.
    CUT TO:

40 INT. BANK. MORNING

Ben waiting in line to cash a cheque. He looks unwell and is having difficulty standing straight. At last it is his turn. He goes to the counter and hands over a cheque to the girl.

> BANK GIRL
OK . . . four thousand, six hundred dollars . . . one moment, sir . . .

She looks at her computer read-out.

. . . that'll leave five dollars in your account. Would you sign the back of the cheque, please?

> BEN
> (*surprised*)
You couldn't cash it just like it is?

> BANK GIRL
> (*puzzled*)
I'm sorry, sir. Is there a problem?

Ben picks up a pen and tries to sign, but his hands are shaking so much that he cannot do it.

> BEN
> (embarrassed)

Well . . . to tell you the truth, I'm a little shaky right now. I just had brain surgery . . . Why don't I come back after lunch, when I'm feeling a little better? We can take care of it then.

He picks up the cheque with some difficulty and exits.
CUT TO:

41 INT. BEN'S BAR. LA. MORNING

Ben seated at the bar, a pile of bills in front of him. The barman sets down a vodka, picks up the empty glass and takes some bills, shaking his head in disapproval. The TV is on, same game show as before, and Ben watches carefully, looking for a sign from the girl, but the show proceeds in its 'normal' fashion. The only difference is that the Hostess is played by the girl in the bank. Ben grabs the Barman's attention.

> BEN

I think, when I'm done with this, I'll have gin and tonic . . . Bombay gin and tonic.

The Barman loses it.

> BARMAN
> (angry)

You should be having coffee. Do you know what time it is? You're a young man.

> (calmer)

It's none of my business, but if you could see what I see, you wouldn't do this to yourself.

Ben is taken aback by the emotion in his voice. In his mind, cynicism and the desire to cry fight it out. He holds the emotion back, and looks down at the bar.

> BEN

I understand what you're saying . . . I appreciate your concern. It's not my intention to make you uncomfortable. Please . . . serve me today and I will never come in here again.

(cheerful)

If I do, you can eighty-six me.

BARMAN

Sure, sure, I can eighty-six you now if I want to. Stop fucking with me. I don't give a fuck what you do.

He picks up a bottle of gin, fills a glass, slams it on the counter in front of Ben and knocks twice with his knuckles on the bar.

On the house, son.

Ben looks at the TV for a sign. None is forthcoming.
CUT TO:

42 INT. BANK. DAY

Ben waiting in line again. The same Bank Girl is there and she is dealing with her customers in the same inanely cheerful way that the game-show Hostess dealt with her prize-winners. She notices Ben waiting and an irritated look flashes across her face. Ben studies her. She is pretty in an ordinary kind of way. We hear Ben's thoughts as voice-over (or maybe he says them out loud to himself).

Are you desirable? Are you irresistible? Maybe if you drank
bourbon with me, it would help. Maybe if you kissed me and I
could taste the sting in your mouth, it would help.

> *Close-up on the Bank Girl as she does her thing, efficiently counting
> money, smiling, perfect teeth framed by a Cupid mouth. She is
> wearing a white blouse through which frilly lingerie can just be made
> out.*

If you drank bourbon with me naked . . . if you smelled of
bourbon as you fucked me, it would help . . . it would increase my
esteem for you. If you poured bourbon on to your naked body and
said to me . . . drink this . . .

> *Camera moves in tighter on her face as she chats with a customer
> about the weather.*

. . . if you spread your legs and had bourbon dripping from your
breasts and your vagina and said drink here . . . then I could fall in
love with you, because then I would have a purpose, to clean you
up, and that would prove that I'm worth something. I'd lick you
clean so that you could go away and fuck someone else.

Next!

Ben takes a moment to come out of his reverie. He smiles and comes to the counter, completely in control of himself.

> **BEN**

I'm back, I've got my cheque . . . and baby . . . I'm ready to sign.

He flips the cheque over, makes sure she is watching and signs with a flourish.

There . . . Steady as a fucking rock, excuse my French.
> (*serious*)

Wanna have dinner with me?

She counts the money out and glares at him as she hands it over.

> **BANK GIRL**

I'm glad you're feeling better. Do you need validation?

Ben looks at her and smiles.
CUT TO:

43 INT. SUPERMARKET. DAY

Ben throws items into a trolley. Garbage bags, firelighters and charcoal lighter fluid.
CUT TO:

44 INT. BEN'S KITCHEN. DAY

Ben putting all the kitchen utensils into a large garbage bag. Three other bags are already filled and the kitchen is looking empty.
CUT TO:

45 INT. BEN'S BEDROOM. DAY

Ben is stuffing all the bedding into a garbage bag. Next he opens a drawer on the dresser and begins taking out clothes and stuffing them into another bag. He pauses for a moment to take a drink from a tall glass.

CUT TO:

46 INT. BEN'S LIVING ROOM. DAY

All the books from the bookcase go into another bag. Then all the records. But he selects certain favourites and as this sequence progresses we see that Ben is making tapes of these tracks. As soon as he is done with the recording, he throws the album into a garbage bag.

CUT TO:

47 EXT. BEN'S YARD. NIGHT

Ben pours lighter fluid on to a pile of photographs and then throws a match on to it. It bursts into flames. He throws more stuff on and the fire blazes. A curious neighbour watches from a safe distance, not wanting to get involved.

ANGLE ON THE FIRE

A watercolor, a poem to his wife, a photograph of him and his wife, a Polaroid of a naked woman, his medical records, his birth and marriage certificates, divorce papers, strips of photographs from booths, postcards from Hawaii. Two small children (his?).

ANGLE ON BEN

34

Now the flames are high and Ben has to stand back as he throws things on to the fire . . . his camera, an engraved box, his wife's 'left behind' clothing, a clock . . .

    CUT TO:

48 EXT. BEN'S HOUSE. DAWN

Fifteen neatly tied garbage bags and Ben's furniture are stacked up on the sidewalk. Ben comes out of his front door carrying a racing bike. He walks to the neighbours' house and places the bike on the porch. We see a label saying 'To Brad from Ben'. He walks to his black car with a small suitcase, gets in and drives off.

    CUT TO:

49 EXT. DESERT LANDSCAPE WITH ROAD. DAY

A high wide shot shows a small black car making its way across the frame.

    DISSOLVE TO:

50 INT. CAR. DAY

Through the window we see a dead straight road stretching to infinity.

The sunlight is painfully bright. On the soundtrack we hear one of Ben's chosen tapes, which continues through into the next shot.
DISSOLVE TO:

51 EXT. GAS STATION IN THE DESERT. DAY

Ben is filling his car. A towncar drives in and stops next to the BMW. Three men get out. They look like Russian Mobsters. Ben nods at them and they nod back.
CUT TO:

52 INT. CAR. NIGHT

Same angle through the window but this time we see Las Vegas at night as Ben drives down the main drag. An overdose of neon.

52A EXT. LAS VEGAS STRIP. NIGHT

Ahead we see the light changing, but Ben doesn't notice until it's almost too late. The car stops and we see Sera crossing in front of the car. She gives Ben a look of real attitude because he is over the line and she has to change course to cross in front.
CUT TO:

53 EXT. HOTEL FORECOURT. NIGHT

Sera is talking to Yuri. A middle-aged man gets out of a cab and Yuri shakes him by the hand and introduces him to Sera. He hands Yuri an envelope and then Sera and he go into the hotel together. Yuri looks around thoughtfully before getting into a cab and driving off.

54 INT. DOCTOR'S OFFICE. DAY

Improvised scene. *

55 INT. MOTEL RECEPTION. NIGHT

Ben waits to check in while the manager explains the house rules to a family of large white people from the Midwest.

*Dialogue for this scene appears in the Afterword.

MANAGER

All rooms to be paid a week in advance, maid service is optional, use of the pool is at your own risk, there is no lifeguard on duty.

Above the manager's head is the name of the motel, The Whole Year Inn. *Ben stares at it and then smiles.*

BEN'S POV

The sign has changed to The Hole You're In.

CUT TO:

56 INT. LIQUOR STORE. NIGHT

Ben has almost filled a trolley with bottles of various brands. He is whistling and seems happy.

57 INT. DOCTOR'S OFFICE. DAY

Improvised scene. ★

CUT TO:

58 EXT. THE STRIP. NIGHT

Ben driving. He sees Sera and follows her, then drives up on the sidewalk. She sees him.

BEN

Hello!

SERA

Hello.

BEN

Are you working?

SERA
(*tough*)

Working? What do you mean, working? I'm walking.

And she walks a few steps to prove it, stopping on the passenger side of his car. They pause for a moment and Ben is confused. He is quite taken with her beauty, but this is not going according to plan. He

★Dialogue for this scene appears in the Afterword.

37

*reaches into the car quickly and picks an open can of beer, draining it
before tossing the empty back on to the rear seat.*

Isn't it illegal to drink and drive?

> **BEN**
> (*laughs*)

That's funny.

> (*seriously*)

I wonder if you'll take two hundred and fifty dollars to fuck me?

Sera doesn't say anything.

That is, if you'll come to my room for an hour, I will give you five
hundred dollars.

> **SERA**

Maybe you shouldn't stand in the road like that. You're pretty
drunk.

He bites his lips as he waits for her to respond.

> (*softer*)

You're pretty drunk.

BEN
(factual)

Not really. My room's not far. The Whole Year Inn. You can drive with me if you want . . .

She makes no response.

. . . or we can walk . . . or I'll give you cab fare.

Takes out his money.

Whatever you want.

She touches the door handle.

SERA

Why don't you give me the money when I'm in the car, and I'll drive with you.

It takes Ben a moment or two to register that she is saying yes. He comes around the car to open the door for her.

BEN

I'm Ben.

They shake hands.

SERA

I'm Sera.

She gets in. Ben gets in.
CUT TO:

59 INT. CAR. NIGHT

Ben hands her the money.

BEN

Sarah – with an H?

SERA

No – S.E.R.A.

They grin at each other.

You wanna start the engine?

They drive off.

60 EXT. MOTEL PARKING LOT. NIGHT

They sit in the car for a while before speaking.

SERA

I'm sort of curious . . . it you're willing to pay me two-fifty . . . not that I mind . . . I mean, I'm OK with that – why aren't you staying in a real hotel?

BEN

We can go to one if you'd prefer.

SERA

No, this is fine. I was just wondering.

Ben switches off the engine but makes no move to get out of the car.

BEN

Well . . . I'm here because I'm a drunk who tends to pass out at odd hours for unpredictable stretches. I'm going to a hotel soon. A room with balcony to pass out on . . . or off.

He falls silent.

SERA

Umm. We can stay in the car for an hour if you want. But I really have to go then. It's your time.

BEN

Right, I'll get your door. I tend to fade in and out lately.

SERA

I guess I do too.

BEN

You what?

SERA

I sometimes fade out.

BEN

Oh . . . well, maybe we better synchronize our spells . . . or stagger them.

SERA
(*gently*)

You were going to get my door.

> *He gets out and she waits for him to open her door. She gets out and he offers her his arm. She takes it and they walk into the motel.*
> CUT TO:

61 INT. BEN'S ROOM. NIGHT

As Ben closes the door, Sera surveys the room.

SERA
(*amused*)

What this room needs . . . is more booze.
SERA'S POV

> *There are bottles everywhere. Ben has gone to a lot of trouble to lay them out in a pleasing way.*

BEN

Do you think so?

> *She turns and looks at him, appraising him. Suddenly she's all business, in control, and Ben likes it.*

SERA

Mind if I use the bathroom?

BEN

Of course.

> *She goes into the bathroom.*

Want a drink? I'm having one.

SERA
(*off-screen*)

A shot of tequila, if you can spare it.

BEN

Of course.

> *Ben smiles, happier than we've ever seen him. He gets her order ready*

41

and then he takes a big swig from a bourbon bottle. He sits on the edge of the bed.

The bathroom door opens and Sera comes in wearing a black bra and panties. She's acting the hooker now, tough and sexy.

SERA

For two-fifty we can do pretty much what you want. You've been drinking, so it might be better if I got on top, but the other way's fine too. I have some jelly in case you want to fuck my ass, that's up to you. If you want to come on my face, that's OK too, just try to keep it out of my hair, I just washed it . . . and my eyes, it stings.

She walks to the table and downs her tequila in one. Then comes to the bed, where Ben is sitting. She kneels, unzips his fly and begins sucking him. Ben watches her, looks at her reflection in the closet mirror, reaches for the bottle and drinks some, being careful not to disturb Sera. After a while Sera comes up.

Do you want to fuck now?

                              BEN
                            (confused)
Maybe another drink first. More tequila?

                              SERA
OK . . . whatever.

She takes the bottle and drinks. She goes down again. Ben stops her.

What's the story? Are you too drunk to come?

                              BEN
                            (sincere)
I don't care about that. There's time left. You can have more
money. You can drink all you want. You can talk or listen. Just
stay, that's all I want.

*She looks at him, confused. She sees a strange look on his face. It
throws her.*

This is a turning point. Both of them are momentarily exposed.

*Ben lifts the sheet and moves to one side, indicating that she should
come into the bed. She's as confused as he is. She gets in with him
and he hands her the bottle.*
CUT TO:

62 INT. CASINO. NIGHT

*Yuri is losing at one of the tables. He continues to bet though, putting
half of what he has left on one number. He loses again. He mops his
face with a red silk handkerchief and places another bet.*

63 INT. SOMEWHERE IN THE CASINO. NIGHT

*The three Russian Mobsters we saw in the desert are walking through
the casino, looking for someone.*
CUT TO:

64 INT. BEN'S ROOM. NIGHT

They are both in bed, drinking.

SERA

So, Ben, what brings you to Las Vegas? Business convention?

They both laugh and Ben hands her the bottle.

BEN

No, I came here to drink . . . myself . . . you know . . .

SERA

To death?

BEN

Yes, that's right.

He looks at her, she at him, not sure whether to believe him or not.

I cashed in all of my money, paid my AmEx card, gonna sell the car tomorrow.

SERA

How long's it gonna take, for you to drink yourself to death?

BEN

I think about four weeks, and I've got enough for about two hundred and fifty to three hundred dollars a day.

SERA

Yes . . . that should do it. What am I? A luxury?

BEN

Yeah. And your meter just ran out.

Ben looks at his watch.

SERA

It's OK . . . nice watch. Go on. Talk some more.

Ben yawns, suddenly deeply tired.

BEN

In LA I kept running out of booze and the store would be closed because I'd forget to look at my watch . . . so I decided to move here because nothing ever closes and because I got tired of getting funny looks when I would walk into a bar at six o'clock . . . even the bartenders started preaching.

(*yawns again*)

44

Here, everyone's from out of town so no one cares, no one is overtly fucking up.

CUT TO:

Later.

SIDE ANGLE

Sera is in focus, Ben is asleep.

> SERA
> (*voice-over*)

I guess I was intrigued by him . . . There was a lot of stuff that I wanted to ask him about but didn't because I didn't want to sound too interested in a trick. But I felt as if a relationship was being forged very quickly.

65 INT. DOCTOR'S OFFICE. DAY

Improvised scene. *

CUT TO:

65A EXT. SERA'S APARTMENT COMPLEX. DAWN

Sera gets out of cab and makes her way towards her apartment, changing out of her high heels as she walks.

66 INT. SERA'S HOUSE. DAWN

Sera lets herself in. Yuri is standing in the shadows. She gets a fright when she sees him.

> YURI

Where have you been?

> SERA

It was a slow night. I went to a hotel for a few drinks.

> *Yuri holds out his hand for her bag. She gives it to him. He finds the money and counts it.*

> YURI

A full night on the street and this is all?

*Dialogue for this scene appears in the Afterword.

45

SERA

Like I said . . . it was a slow night . . . I'm sorry. It was hard to score.

Yuri slaps her.

Don't hit me.

YURI

What do you think . . . you are sixteen years old on Hollywood Boulevard?

Yuri talks in Russian, becoming angrier, and slaps her again. He spits on the floor.

Sera falls against the kitchen table and picks up a lethal-looking knife. Yuri stops.

SERA

Maybe nobody wants to fuck a chick with a cut on her cheek.

She throws the knife to Yuri, who catches it. She bends over the table and pulls up her skirt.

There, go ahead!

She mimics him.

A shower of Russian comes out of Yuri, but he doesn't touch her. He tries to regain his dignity by putting on a coat.

YURI

I could kill you. You know that.

He goes to the door.

Work, tonight, bring me money, no matter the hour.

And he exits. Sera is still on the table.

SERA

I will, Yuri. I will.
CUT TO:

46

67 INT. PAWN SHOP. DAY

The proprietor is handing over some cash to Yuri, whose jewellery is on the counter. He pockets it and as he turns to leave, Ben comes in. They pass without taking much notice of each other. Ben removes his Rolex and shows it to the man.

CUT TO:

68 EXT. STREET. LAS VEGAS. DAY

Yuri is walking in the hot sun, sweating. We see him through long-lens heat haze. The camera wanders into the traffic and we see the black towncar crawling along behind him, the three men inside.

CUT TO:

69 INT. DOCTOR'S OFFICE. DAY

Improvised scene. *

CUT TO:

70 INT. MAIN BAR. HOTEL. NIGHT

A lounge singer belts out a fair rendition of a Tony Orlando number. Sera sits at the bar, an empty seat on either side of her. She watches a younger hooker in the final moments of pulling a dangerous-looking man. The girl is aware of Sera without even looking at her. The guy she is with looks around and sees Sera. The girl shoots her an icy look. A man sits next to Sera: a conventioneer.

> CONVENTIONEER
About ready for another drink?

> SERA
Yes, that would be great. Are you here for the convention?

> CONVENTIONEER
Do I look that obvious? My name's Paul.

They shake hands.

> SERA
No, of course not, just a wild guess. I'm Sera and that's a Margarita.

*Dialogue for this scene appears in the Afterword.

The Barman is already pouring. The young hooker leaves with her dangerous guy. She pauses long enough to give Sera a nasty smile. The conventioneer pays for the drink and is a little lost for words. Sera tries to help.

So . . . are you alone, or are you just using me to make someone else jealous?

> CONVENTIONEER
> (*laughs nervously*)

Alone. Alone. I'm here alone.

> SERA
> (*friendly*)

Where are you staying?

> CONVENTIONEER
> (*suspicious*)

Right here in the hotel. Why?

> SERA
> (*moving a little closer*)

Well . . . I thought you might be looking for a date.

> CONVENTIONEER
> (*shocked*)

A date. What, are you a hooker?
> (*voice getting louder*)

What do you mean a date?
> (*and louder*)

I've got a wife back home. I just came over to talk for a few minutes.

> SERA
> (*quietly*)

I'm sorry, I guess I misunderstood.

She looks around.

Please don't raise your voice. I won't bother you about it again.

> CONVENTIONEER
> (*calmer*)

Sorry. Look . . . you seem like a nice girl. I'm just sick of everyone in this town trying to get my money.

He gets up.

Here, have another drink. I gotta go.

He leaves. Sera is uncomfortable. People watch her, aware that something has been going on. The Barman comes over to where Sera is sitting. He speaks quietly, not unfriendlily.

BARMAN
Maybe you should give it a miss for this evening.

He walks away. Sera finishes her drink and leaves.
CUT TO:

71 EXT. THE STRIP. NIGHT

Sera at work is looking more carefully than usual, hoping to see Ben.

A huge silver limo pulls up and, after some negotiation, she gets in.
CUT TO:

72 EXT. THE STRIP. NIGHT

Long-lens shot of Ben, very drunk on the street. He falls and lies still for quite a long time before getting up. He falls into the road and tries to hail a cab, but none stops. A cop car cruises to a halt and Ben more or less imitates a normal person as he walks out of shot.

73 EXT. THE POOL. MOTEL. DAY

Ben dives in and swims a length under water. He pulls himself out and sits next to the large Midwestern family. The father says hello and introduces his family to Ben. They are all very friendly. It's a nice atmosphere around this pool and for a moment Ben even looks healthy.
CUT TO:

74 EXT. THE STRIP. NIGHT

A limo pulls up and Sera gets out. She sees something.
SERA'S POV

Ben sitting at a bus stop, drinking out of a cocktail glass. When he sees her he gets up, a little unsteadily.

BEN

I couldn't remember what happened last time. I was afraid that I might have been rude, or mean to you.

He looks at her.

If I was, I'm sorry.

SERA

No, just drunk . . . but that's OK. Where's your car?

BEN

I sold it this morning. I'm going to take cabs from now on in.

Sera looks up and down the strip.

Don't run away.

SERA
(*defensive*)

Why should I? I know you're not a cop, so what is it tonight? Another two-fifty to watch you sleep?

Ben sits back down, a little hurt.

What's up?

BEN

I was looking for you tonight. I don't know if you have a boyfriend . . .

He thinks.

or a girlfriend, but if you have some free time . . . maybe we could . . . have dinner.

SERA
(*tough again, but pleased*)

Are you serious?

BEN
(*deadly serious*)

I think you know I'm serious. I'll pay you if you like . . . but I'd like to see you.

SERA

No, I can't have dinner with you.

And she hails a taxi, which stops immediately and she gets in.

The Mojave Hotel, please.

Ben watches the cab drive off.
CUT TO:

75 INT. CORRIDOR OF HOTEL. NIGHT

Sera walks along, checking numbers on doors. She finds the right one and knocks firmly.

YURI
(*voice-over*)

Yes? What?

SERA

It's me, Yuri.

The door opens a crack and Yuri peers out.

YURI

Sera! It's . . .

He looks around for a clock.

. . . it's late.

76 INT. YURI'S ROOM. NIGHT

Sera comes into the room, takes her purse out and counts out seven hundred dollars.

SERA

Sorry, Yuri . . . good night . . . lots of tricks . . . I think things are picking up.

Yuri sits on the bed. He looks unwell and disoriented. His face is covered with a thin film of sweat. He seems to be listening for something, because he stops her talking by putting his fingers to his lips. He looks at her and then beckons her to the bed. Sera is nervous. As she walks to the bed, she begins unbuttoning her blouse. Yuri stops

her with a wave of his hand. Sera is puzzled and frightened now.
Yuri seems to be deranged.

YURI

Have you told anyone that I'm here?

SERA

No.

Yuri suddenly hears something. He grabs Sera's hand and takes her
to the wall. He presses her head to the wall.

YURI

Do you hear that?

He looks at her.

They're talking about me.

He pulls himself together.

Go, Sera.

(whispers)

Go. Stay at home. I will call you tomorrow.

52

SERA

Yuri . . . are you . . .

YURI
(*patiently*)

Sera . . . please go.

He indicates the wall.

This is very important . . . and I must listen. Now go.

They face each other for a moment and then Yuri does an almost comic gesture to tell her to go. He hustles her to the door and shoves her out as she is still buttoning up her blouse. He slams the door.

(*through the door*)

Goodbye, Sera. Don't come back here. I will not see you again.

Sera stands there for a while, almost in shock, and then she begins to walk. The camera follows her as she makes her way down the endless corridor of doors. Ahead of her, three men are walking towards her, checking the door numbers as they make their way. Sera doesn't take them in. They pass and turn a corner. We recognize them as the men from the black towncar.

ANGLE

The men have stopped outside Yuri's room. The camera pans and we see Sera down the other corridor getting into the elevator.

FADE OUT:

77 INT. BEN'S ROOM AT THE MOTEL. NIGHT

Ben is lying on the bed watching a game show, drinking.

A coughing fit hits him. He is very short of breath. We see how ill he really is.

There is a tap at the door.

BEN

No thanks . . . I'm fine.

The tapping persists and eventually Ben gets off the bed and unlocks it, but keeps the chain on. It is Sera.

53

Still want to have dinner?

Ben stares at her for a while.

Yes.

I have to change and take a shower first. If you want to come home and wait.

Ben opens the door.

We should pick up a bottle of tequila on the way. I owe you one.

You do?

CUT TO:

78 INT. SERA'S HOUSE. NIGHT

Sera is finishing in the shower and Ben is sitting at the kitchen table. He gets up and walks around the house, trying to get a sense of her. The furniture is very plain and there is a spartan quality about the house. He looks with interest at the bookshelf, which has a good selection of literature.

(to himself)

This is the home of an angel.

(off-screen)

You OK out there?

Yes. Take your time. I'm fine.

He pours himself another drink.

(off-screen)

Pour yourself another drink.

He sits down and she comes in, towelling her hair.

You OK?

> BEN

Of course. Wow . . . you look extremely beautiful.

> SERA

Thank you. What time is it?

> BEN

Don't know. My watch went the way of the car.

He holds up his empty wrist for her to see. Then looks up and sees her watching him.

I'm rambling. I really like you. You make me want to talk . . . I don't know what time it is.

> SERA

I like hearing you talk.
> (*businesslike*)

If you feel up to a short walk, there's a place to eat around the corner. All the food in Vegas is terrible so the place doesn't really matter. How does that sound to you?

> BEN

Do they have drinks?
> CUT TO:

79 EXT. THE STRIP. NIGHT

Ben and Sera walk and talk.

80 INT. RESTAURANT. NIGHT

Ben and Sera are eating. He plays with his food, eating very little of it. Finally he pushes it away and orders another drink.

> SERA

I'm from the East. I went to college, did an arts course. I now live in Vegas. I think of it as home. I came here deliberately to carve out a life. I was in LA before, but I'll come back to that later.
> (*pause*)

The tough times are behind me now. I can deal with the bad things that happen. There will always be dark characters. But my life is good. It is as I would want it to be. So, why are you drunk?

BEN

Is that really what you want to ask me?

SERA

Yes.

BEN
(*worried*)

Well, then I guess this is our first date . . . or our last. Until now, I wasn't sure it was either.

SERA

Very clever.

Sera thinks for a while and decides to give in to him on this.

First. It's our first. I'm just concerned. So . . . why are you killing yourself?

BEN

Interesting choice of words. I don't remember. I just know that I want to.

SERA

Want to what? Kill yourself? Are you saying that you're drinking as a way to kill yourself?

And she leans across the table to be close to him, listening intently. Ben becomes uncomfortable and tries to joke it off.

BEN

Or killing myself as a way to drink.

Sera continues to stare at him, wanting to know the real answer. He takes a slug from his drink. She sits back.

We'll talk about it some other time maybe. OK?

Sera relaxes and continues with her food. We hear her thoughts for a moment.

SERA
(*voice-over*)

It wasn't so important to me. I mean, he never asked me why I was a hooker, and that was impressive. I really liked him. So I decided to just play my part. I mean . . . it's good to help someone once in a while, it's a bonus to being alive, and that was my plan . . . to stay alive. I suddenly came to a decision.

BEN

What are you thinking? Are you angry with me?

SERA
(*decides something*)

Ben, why don't you stay at my place tonight? I mean . . . look, you're so drunk. I like you. I trust you.

BEN

That's astonishing. Sera, look . . .

SERA

I hate to think of you in that cheesy motel. I mean . . .

And she folds her arms and grins at him.

Let's face it, what the fuck are you doing in Las Vegas?

BEN
(*overwhelmed by her*)

I'm going to move to a smart hotel, tomorrow if it'll make you feel better.
(*looks at her*)
Let's talk about tomorrow. Wanna do something?

SERA
(*warmly*)

Sure . . . tonight. Then please stay at my place.

BEN

Sera . . . you know I'm not much good in the sack.

SERA

It's not about sex, Ben. I'll make you up a bed on the sofa. Do it for me. We can talk till late and then sleep till late. As you know, I am my own boss.

57

Ben laughs loud, the most animated we've seen him, and his laugh is infectious, and Sera joins in. Other diners turn to stare at them. They seem like a couple.

CUT TO:

81 EXT. THE STRIP. NIGHT

Ben and Sera walk and talk, holding hands.

82 EXT. DESERT. DAY

A wide shot. The black towncar makes its way across frame. Left to right.

CUT TO:

83 INT. SERA'S HOUSE. DAY

Ben is asleep on the sofa. As he wakes up, he becomes aware that Sera is watching him from across the room. They smile at each other.

> BEN

How long have I been here?

> SERA

Three nights, two days. When is your rent coming up at the motel?

> BEN

I don't know.

> (*sits up*)

I'll go and sort it out today. Why don't you come? . . . We'll find a real room for me. You can pick it out, a tower on the strip.

> SERA

There's no reason to blow all your money on a hotel room.

> BEN

What do you mean?

> SERA

What I mean is that you should bring your stuff over here. We're spending all this time together . . . what the fuck!

BEN

Sera . . .

SERA

Let's face it, Ben, we're having fun here. I've never done so much talking in my life.

BEN

Me neither.

SERA

So! Let's dispense with the formalities. I want you here . . . now!

BEN

Sera . . . you are crazy.

SERA

So . . . I'm not too concerned with long-term plans.

BEN

Don't you think you'll get a little bored living with a drunk?

SERA

That is what I want. Why don't you go and get your stuff?

BEN

You haven't seen the worst of it. These last few days I've been very controlled. I knock things over . . . I throw up all the time.
(looks at her)
Now I feel really good . . . You're like some kind of antidote that mixes with the liquor and keeps me in balance, but that won't last forever. You'll get tired of it really quickly. Believe me.

They sit in silence for a while.

SERA

OK, you go back to your hotel and I'll go back to my glamorous life of being alone.

She walks out of the room, and into the bathroom, where she sits on the toilet to pee.

(to herself)
The only thing I have to come home to is a bottle of Listerine to wash the taste of come out of my mouth. I'm tired of being

alone . . . that's what I'm tired of.

She finishes, wipes herself and flushes the toilet. Pulling up her panties, she walks back into the bedroom, where Ben is putting on his shoes.

Don't you like me, Ben?

BEN
(devastated)

Don't be silly.

Ben is unable to deal with the fact that he is absolutely in love with her. He walks out of the room. She follows.

SERA

We gotta decide this . . . right now. Before we go any further. You either stay here with me or . . .

Ben turns to look at her.

we can't see each other any more.

Ben and Sera look at each other for a long time.

BEN

Sera . . . what you don't understand is . . .

SERA

What?

Ben is deeply troubled. He comes to a decision.

BEN

You can never . . . never . . . ask me to stop drinking. Do you understand?

SERA
(dead serious)

I do. I really do.

(smiles)

OK. I have to do some shopping alone. You go out for a few drinks and then pick up your things. Don't hurry and I'll be back before you to let you in.

Sera grabs him in a big embrace that knocks him off his balance and into the wall. She kisses him all over his face and squeezes his skinny frame.
CUT TO:

84 INT. BEN'S ROOM AT THE MOTEL. DAY

Ben is packing his liquor into his suitcase. The almost-empty bottles he pours into a large cup, which he drinks from. The suitcase is now full and Ben suddenly realizes that he hasn't packed any clothes. They are all in a pile on the bed. He talks to himself.

BEN
Maybe this isn't a good idea after all.

He tries to put clothes in with the bottles, but the lid won't close. He sits on the bed and has an imaginary conversation with Sera.

Listen, angel . . . the thing is that I'm nuts about you and this is a bad thing . . . because my real plan is to die here and you were never even part of my plan . . . but like I said, I am nuts about you . . . wait a minute, I have an idea, angel.

And he opens the closet and finds some plastic laundry bags, which he puts his clothes in.

86 EXT. SERA'S HOUSE. DAY

Sera's neighbours, a husband and wife, are standing outside her house. They stop her. They are also her landlord.

HUSBAND

We didn't know whether to call the police or not.

And they indicate the sleeping figure of Ben, in the doorway, clutching a bottle of bourbon, using his suitcase as a pillow.

WIFE

He's been there for about half an hour. My husband thought he'd seen you two together, but I thought it best to wait until you got home.

SERA

Yes, he's my friend. I guess he had just a little too much to drink
           (smiling uncomfortably)
I'll help him inside.
           (puts down her packages)
Thanks for your concern. Sorry to trouble you.

HUSBAND
(gallantly)

Well, call me if there's anything I can do.

They go to their own house. Sera opens the front door, kneels down next to Ben and shakes him gently.

SERA

Can you wake up?

Ben opens his eyes and looks around with a pleasant, cheerful expression.

BEN

Hi!

SERA

Why don't you go in and sit down. I have some gifts for you.

BEN

Right . . . OK . . .

Ben stands and almost loses his balance. He picks up his suitcase and attempts to pick up her packages as well, but she stops him.

SERA

Don't worry . . . I got 'em.

Ben staggers in with his case. As Sera enters, she looks around and sees Husband and Wife at the window, still watching.

BEN
(*off-screen*)

Want a drink? Great nap. Wanna go out tonight?

SERA

Seriously, Ben . . . I need to keep pretty low-key around here. Maybe next time you could nap this side of the door. That was the landlord.

BEN

Oh, I always do. Don't worry. I'm sorry about that, but I got back too early and the door was locked.

SERA

Of course . . .

She reaches into her purse.

Gift number one.

And she gives him a newly cut key. He takes it and tries it in the lock, then drops it into his pocket.

BEN

I used to carry a lot of keys, but one by one they all fell victim to the great condensation. Now I have just this one . . . which is . . .

And he tails off and stares at the floor. She waits for him to continue and then comes to him and touches him on the arm.

                              SERA

Ben?

                              BEN

Sorry.

He shakes his head.

I was miles away,

He sees the parcels.

Ah . . . more gifts. I have to sit down for this.

He strides into the living room and flops on to the sofa. She follows.

Sera, I love that name . . . S.E.R.A. Before we proceed onwards,
there is something I need to say. OK?

                              SERA

OK.

                              BEN

I've come this far . . . here I am, in your house. I want you to let
me pay your rent for this month. All right?

*And he stares at her as if to say that nothing can happen until this
matter is resolved.*

                              SERA

Why?

                              BEN

Because . . . it's better for me that way. OK?

                              SERA

Well . . . OK . . .

She is uncomfortable.

They sit in silence for a while.

                              BEN

Sera . . . I hope that you understand how I feel about this. First of
all, you're welcome to my money. We can buy a couple of cases of

liquor and you can have the rest. But I don't think you're talking to me right now about money.

SERA
(*smiling*)

No?

BEN

No. I think you're talking about you. I'll tell you right now that I'm in love with you . . . but, be that as it may, I'm not here to force my twisted life into your soul.

SERA

I know that . . .

BEN

. . . and I'm not here to demand your attention to the point where it changes your life. We know I'm a drunk . . . but that seems to be all right with you. And I know that you're a hooker. I hope you understand that I'm a person who is totally at ease with this . . . which is not to say that I'm indifferent or that I don't care . . . I do . . . it simply means that I trust and accept your judgement. What I'm saying is . . . that I hope you understand that I understand.

SERA

Thanks, I do understand. I was worried about how that would be . . . but now I'm not. And you should know that included with the rent around here is a complimentary blow job.

BEN

Ah, yes . . . I suppose sooner or later we ought to fuck.

SERA

Whatever that means. Open your presents.

She hands him the larger of the two parcels.

Open this one first.

Ben awkwardly unwraps the present, a large, colourful shirt. A genuine smile comes on to his face.

BEN

Very nice.

65

He holds the shirt against himself.

This should work very nicely with my suit, which, by the way, is the only item of clothing I brought over from the motel with me.

Sera raises an eyebrow.

SERA

Right . . . the suitcase was clinking. So what did you do with your clothes?

BEN
(laughing)

I threw them into the garbage, which was perhaps immoral, but I wanted to come to you clean, so to speak. I thought we could go shopping and pick up a pair of jeans and forty-five pairs of underwear and just throw them out each day.

SERA
(smiling)

Nice talk, Ben. Keep drinking. In between the hundred and one proof breath and the occasional drool, some interesting words fall from your mouth.

She hands him the last present.

Now, try this one.

Ben unwraps the smaller gift. It is a silver hip flask. He is very touched and a little tear trickles down his cheek.

BEN

Well . . . looks like I'm with the right girl.

He turns it in his hands.

I must say that I'm very impressed that you would buy this for me. I know you wouldn't do this without thinking about it. Funny . . . you did just what I would have done.

Ben stands and tries the flask in his pocket for fit. It is fine. He walks to the door.

I'm going to fill it right now.

SERA

Do you want to go gambling tonight? We could go out and play for a few hours.

Ben comes back into the room, takes the flask out of his suit pocket and has a drink.

BEN

I hadn't planned to gamble . . . but if you would keep the bulk of my money here, then I could safely blow a couple of hundred bucks.

He takes out all of his money, peels off a few hundreds and then gives her the rest.

Giving you money makes me want to come.

SERA

Then come.
(pause)
I'm going to change. Watch TV. I'll be half an hour.

And she leaves. There is a slight edge to her voice and Ben is not sure if he offended her or not. He watches through the small angle of the door as she changes.

I am planning to go out and do some work.

SERA

BEN

When?

SERA

Tomorrow night as a matter of fact.

88 EXT. THE STRIP. NIGHT

Ben and Sera walking. The camera follows them. He is wearing his new shirt and looks good in it. She is wearing a green dress and mismatched earrings and looks great. They walk and talk.

BEN

I like your earrings.

He changes sides.

I like women who wear mismatched earrings.

SERA

Well, then . . . I hope we don't run into any tonight.

BEN
(laughs)

What do you mean?

SERA

I expect some kind of loyalty here. Just because I fuck for money doesn't give you cause to start picking up women and leaving me looking silly.

And she stops and looks at him, smiling but serious.

BEN

And I only have eyes for you. And we both know that you would never become romantically involved with a trick, right?

89 INT. CASINO. NIGHT

They walk around the huge space, which is full of people and energy, and suddenly Ben grabs Sera and pushes her against a slot machine and kisses her deeply. At first she resists and then she gives in to him and responds. They knock over some change, which falls to the floor, and

Ben pulls away from her for a beat to bend down and scoop up all the change and hand it to the bemused player, before returning to Sera's mouth for more. They break for air and then Ben leads her towards the bar. As he waves to attract the barman's attention, she squeezes his arm.

SERA
(*quietly*)

I love you.

> *But he doesn't hear her.*
> ANGLE ON CASINO ACTIVITY
>
> *On long lens we see Ben and Sera at the bar. Suddenly Ben seems to fall asleep. Sera tries to wake him and then he goes crazy and falls backwards off his stool, knocking a waitress and her drinks over. Security Guards appear and begin arguing with Sera.*
> CUT TO:

90 INT. SARA'S HOUSE. NIGHT

Ben wakes up on the sofa, fully dressed. A night-light gives a soft glow. He rolls off the sofa, landing on all fours on the floor. He crawls to the kitchen, opens the fridge door and takes out a vodka bottle and carton of orange juice. With difficulty he gets to his feet, finds a glass and pours a drink. He swallows the mix and then stands over the sink just in case he has to vomit.

91 INT. SERA'S BEDROOM. NIGHT

Sera wakes and Ben comes in and gets into bed with her.

SERA

How are you doing?

BEN

Very well . . . umm . . . I never expected to have to ask this again . . . but how did our evening go? I remember getting to the casino . . . I remember kissing you . . . that was really nice but everything after that is a blank.

SERA

Well – I was prepared for worse, but it wasn't so bad. We were sitting at the bar, talking about blackjack. You seemed just fine, a little drunker than usual, but nothing really strange, but then your head started to droop and I put my arm on your shoulder and then, wham, you swung your arm at me, and fell backwards off your stool into a cocktail waitress. You smashed everything on her tray, it was a real mess. You kept yelling and yelling.

BEN

Oh. What did you do?

SERA

I tried to shut you up and help you to your feet but you kept swinging at me – not like you wanted to hit me, but more just waving me away. Security came and when you saw them you stopped yelling. They wanted to carry you out and dump you on the street, but I talked them into letting me walk you out.

BEN

That's impressive. How did you do that?

SERA

I told them you were an alcoholic and I would take you home. I also promised that we would never come in there again.

We?

SERA

Yes, we.

BEN

(*holds her hand*)

What happened then?

SERA

You were OK for a while, so we walked for about a block and then you said you wanted to go home and fuck, but I think even you knew that wasn't going to happen. We got a cab and you asked him to stop at a liquor store, even though I told you that we had plenty at home. In the store you gave the kid a hundred and told him to keep the change. I asked you if you knew it was a hundred. You said you did, so I let you do it. We got here, you fell asleep on the couch and I covered you up and came to bed.

BEN

I warned you . . .

(*kisses her hand*)

. . . but I'm sorry.

SERA

Here's my speech . . .

(*kisses his hand*)

. . . I know this shouldn't be acceptable to me, but it is. Don't ask my why. I sense that your trouble is very big . . . and I'm scared for you . . . and so I'm doing what I think you need me to do. Falling down in casinos is little stuff. It doesn't bother me. It has nothing to do with us.

BEN

That's amazing. What are you? Some sort of angel visiting me from one of my drunk fantasies? How can you be so good?

She turns away to the wall and curls up like a small girl.

SERA

I don't know what you're saying. I'm just using you. I need you. Can we not talk about it any more, please. Not another word.

71

He thinks about this. He gently pushes her until she is lying on her front and then he pulls her up her nightdress and stokes her naked back. He kisses her in the small of her back.

                         BEN
Why don't you go back to sleep. I'll go out and buy us some breakfast.

                         SERA
Be careful.

He stands and goes to the door.

                         BEN
Don't worry.

As he leaves the room, she calls after him.

                         SERA
Ben, I'm working tonight.

He opens the door and smiles at her.

                         BEN
I know.
    CUT TO:

92 EXT. SIDEWALK. EARLY MORNING

Ben gets out of his cab and walks up to the doorway of a grocery store. It is locked. Ben looks at his wrist and then remembers that he no longer has a watch. He looks around, sees something and exits frame.
    CUT TO:

93 INT. ROUGH ENGLISH BAR. EARLY MORNING

Ben enters and makes his way to the bar. This is a dirty, dark place. An ageing blonde in leather hot pants is dancing by herself at the juke-box. A very drunk Biker Couple argue noisily in a corner, slurring their words. There is not much gambling taking place at the eight slot machines. Ben sits at the bar and the Bartender slaps down a paper napkin.

A beer and a double kamikaze please.

Sure thing. Anything to eat?

Not quite yet. First I have to drink myself sober, then . . . a few crackers, maybe an egg and toast . . .

The Bartender walks away to get Ben's drinks, Ben continues anyway.

. . . then I'll go home with the groceries and we'll have breakfast together, and that'll make her feel better about my condition . . .

Ben is interrupted by the arrival of the Biker Girl. She is young, tough and pretty. She puts an arm around him and presses against him.

Who the fuck are you talking to, Mr?
(*laughing*)
Why are you all dressed up, honey? My, don't you look fine.

She runs her tongue around her mouth.

I am very bored with my date. Would you like to buy me a drink?

Ben looks around and sees the Biker staring at the two of them.

(*loudly*)
Do you mind if I buy her a drink?

Fuck her. I don't care what the fuck you do with her.

Maybe I could buy you both a drink?

Fuck you. Don't fuck with me, motherfucker. Fuck off. Go to it, she's waiting for her drink.

The Biker walks over to the slot machines and begins dropping in quarters, never taking his eyes off Ben and the Girl.

BIKER GIRL

See what an asshole he is.
(*big smile*)
I'll have a rum and Coke.

BEN

Barman? A rum and Coke please.

The Girl leans with her back to the bar, closer to Ben, who is facing the bar on a stool. She brings her face closer to his.

BIKER GIRL

Can I stay with you for a while?

BEN

You mean move in with me? Isn't this a bit sudden?

BIKER GIRL

Oh, I don't have a lot of stuff.

BEN

(*smiling*)
I don't think my wife would dig it too much.

She moves to his ear to whisper.

BIKER GIRL

Maybe we could just go find a room and fuck all day. You wouldn't have to tell your wife about that, would you? I could suck you like this.

And she begins sucking on his lobe. Behind them, at the slot machine, the Biker is still watching. His face fills with a drunken rage.

BEN

See, the thing is . . . fucking you would be wonderful, but I am deeply in love with Sera . . .

The Biker throws down his beer can and walks towards the bar.

. . . and it's almost impossible for me to imagine being with someone else . . .

The Biker arrives at the bar and grabs Ben.

Now listen, asshole, I'm not gonna just sit around and watch her suck on your ear.

The Biker is about to hit Ben then holds back. He leans in and puts his face next to Ben's.

Now, I know that she came over to you, like she does, so I'm gonna pretend that you're innocent and give you one chance to walk out of this place . . . right now.

BIKER GIRL
(*to Biker*)

Get lost, jerk.

The Biker slaps her and then grabs Ben by the collar.

BIKER

What do you say?

Ben shakes his arm free from the Biker's grip. He thinks about it for a couple of beats and then decides.

BEN

I'm sorry . . . but she and I have decided to spend a few hours together in a mo –

The Biker headbutts Ben in the face, sending him crashing off his stool to the floor. His head cracks against the tiled floor. The Biker walks over to him, picks him up by his shirt front and punches him in the nose. Blood sprays on to his face. The Biker walks out of the bar. The Girl follows him quickly. The Bartender takes a wet towel and walks over to where Ben is struggling to get up, holding his face.

BARTENDER

You're quite a fighter.

He gives him the towel.

This may sound silly, but I'm going to have to ask you to leave. It's what we do around here when there's a fight. Men's room is around the back.

CUT TO:

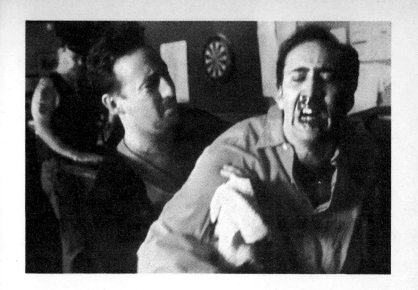

94 EXT. SERA'S HOUSE. MORNING

Ben lets himself in with his key. He is carrying a big bag of groceries. His clothes are bloodstained. The Landlady watches from poolside.

BEN

I'm back.

He walks into the living room and finds Sera reading on the couch. She looks up and sees his face and his bloodstained shirt.

SERA

Oh, no! Oh, fuck, Ben, look at your face. You get in a fight? I thought you didn't fight. Goddammit. How do you feel? Wait here. Sit down.

She goes to the bathroom and we hear her rummaging in the medicine cabinet.

(off-screen)

Did you stop at a bar?

She comes back into the room, armed with bottles and cotton wool.

Did you say something stupid to someone stupid?

She goes to work on his face, dabbing an open cut with some mercurochrome.

BEN

Absolutely not . . . ow . . . I was defending the honour of some poor wayward maiden.

She thinks about this for a moment and then kisses him on the forehead.

SERA

Why don't you go and finish this in the bathroom. Take a shower and put on your other shirt. I'll fix breakfast and then we'll go shopping and get some new clothes. I think this suit must be unlucky.

CUT TO:

INT. MALL. DAY

Ben and Sera come out of a clothing store. Ben is wearing black jeans, red socks and a white dress shirt. They go up the 'up' escalator.

> SERA

Very creative. Now we can get you a black bow tie and you can look like one of those casino dealers.

> BEN

OK, but remember that they wear it because they have to. I wear it because I want to. That'll make me look different. Let's get a drink.

> *Ben somehow gets on to the 'down' escalator, leaving Sera on the higher level.*

> SERA

Ben?

CUT TO:

96 INT. SHOPPING MALL BAR. DAY

Ben needs a drink badly but this is not the best place. Mothers with children, old people and a Waitress with attitude. Ben tries to order but becomes angry when she doesn't bring it straight away. People begin staring. At the next table a dignified older man sits alone.

Ben hands Sera a small package.

CLOSE ANGLE

> BEN

There was no time for me to write a card, with you breathing down my neck all day, so you'll just have to wing it, baby.

> *He laughs and this induces a coughing fit. He downs his drink and holds up the empty glass to let the waitress know she should bring another.*

Open it.

> *She does so. It is a pair of onyx earrings. Black onyx set in white gold.*

SERA
(*pleased*)

Your colour.

BEN

I think you should wear one at a time. One of these . . . and one of
your others. In fact, I was going to buy just one, but I didn't think
it would fly . . . as a gift, I mean.

His new drink arrives and he takes a swallow straight away.

SERA

I'll wear them tonight . . . one of them.

*She looks at him, aware of what she has said, wondering how he is
reacting. She smiles and Ben takes a deep swallow, finishing his
drink. His mood suddenly changes.*

BEN

Yes . . . tonight. Put it on.

She does so. Ben helps her, bringing his face down close to hers.

You'll be able to feel it, sharp and hot under your ear, as one of
the brothers is driving your head, face down into one of the
penthouse pillows.

*They are both suddenly deeply shocked by what he has said. They sit
in silence for a while. Sera is close to tears. Ben gets up suddenly, puts
down a couple of bills and walks away from the table. When he is
almost at the door Sera gets up and quickly tries to gather up all of
the packages.*

SERA

Ben, wait . . . please wait for me.

ANGLE ON THE DOOR

*The dignified older Man stands in Ben's path and places his hands
on Ben's shoulders.*

MAN

Maybe you should wait for her, sir.

BEN

Why?

                                  MAN
Because . . . you can hear in her voice that she really wants you to.

*Sera catches up and the Man lets go of Ben. Ben takes the packages
from Sera and the two of them step out into the mall.*

97 INT. MALL. DAY

They walk together.

                                  SERA
What was that all about?

                                  BEN
Can we just forget it?

                                  SERA
I don't understand any of that.

                                  BEN
Can we just ignore it?

*They stop and look at each other. The PA system gives out an inane
message.*

Please!

                                  SERA
Yes . . . I'll give you that.

                                  BEN
Thank you, Sera.

                                  SERA
Do you want me not to go tonight?

                                  BEN
No . . . we already talked about that.
    CUT TO:

98 INT. SERA'S BEDROOM. NIGHT

*Sera is preparing for work. In the background we can hear the TV next
door. She dresses carefully. Black underwear, stockings, heels, a tight
black skirt.*

82

99 INT. LIVING ROOM. NIGHT

Ben is watching TV and drinking.

100 INT. SERA'S BEDROOM. NIGHT

Sera at the mirror, putting on her make-up. Her make-up is more pronounced than we have seen it before. Everything is more extreme.

101 INT. LIVING ROOM. NIGHT

Sera comes into the room. Ben looks up at her and sucks in his breath.

                                    BEN
Wow.

She walks over to him and takes his head and places it between her breasts and kisses the top of his head.

Maybe I should follow you around and ask one of your tricks what it's like to sleep with you.

                              SERA
They wouldn't know.

She comes on to him.

Maybe you should ask me sometime. I'd be happy to show you.

She goes to the door.

I'll be back home around three. If you're back by then we can watch TV or something . . . I guess what I'm saying is . . . that I hope you are back when I get home. Please be careful.

                              BEN
You be careful too. I'm going to miss you.

                              SERA
Shall we go away for a couple of days?

                              BEN
Yeah . . . I'd like that.
   CUT TO:

102 INT. SMART HOTEL. NIGHT

Sera walks through the lobby, looking for business.

103 EXT. A STREET. NIGHT

Ben lying down with people walking past and over him.
   ANGLE ON BEN'S FACE

A big smile appears on his face. He starts to laugh.
   FADE OUT:

   FADE IN:

104 EXT. DESERT. DAY
A blue car drives across frame. The sun is bright.

105 EXT. DESERT MOTEL. POOL. DAY

Sera is a very good swimmer and we see that Ben must have been quite an athlete. They look at each other under water. They're under water for a long time. Ben exhales. Sera pushes him towards the surface.

Ben and Sera come to the surface. Ben has swallowed water and has a coughing fit. Sera hugs him until the fit passes. The camera moves in tighter on them and music gives the moment a strange chill.

SERA
Don't do that to me. Don't frighten me like that.

CUT TO:

106 EXT. POOL. NIGHT

Ben and Sera are watching the TV next to the pool. They are sitting in reclining chairs. In the distance a coyote howls.

SERA
Years ago, in LA, I turned a trick on Sunset and Western. The guy was polite and didn't argue about the price. He parked his car and I took him to a house that I had an arrangement with. A fat Mexican woman was watching a TV and I told him to give her the twenty for the room. There were three or four small naked children playing on the floor and we had to step over them to get into the room. The room had a bed and a dresser. He lay on his back on the bed and I put a rubber on him and sucked him for a while until he was hard and then I eased on to him. About twenty minutes later there was a knock on the door and it was the woman saying our time was up. I felt kind of guilty because he hadn't come and I offered to reason with the woman and get another ten minutes, but he said it was all right and began dressing. When we were ready to leave the room he stopped me and . . . hugged me and kissed me on the cheek. He gave me an extra hundred as a tip and went back to his car. I remember being relieved that I wouldn't have to work again that evening.

BEN
Last spring I happened to walk past a house that I had once patronized. There was a cool breeze blowing off the ocean and through the window I could see a bare leg. The girl must have

85

been taking a break between customers. It was a strange moment for me because it reminded me of my mother and despite the fact that I was late for something already I just stayed there, loving the atmosphere of it and my memory and . . . the reason I'm telling you this epilogue is that I felt that I'd come full circle.

                              SERA
Where was that house? The one in LA, I mean.

                              BEN
Fifth and Mayflower. You know it?

                              SERA
Yes. One of my friends was there. I wonder if you ever clipped her.

They watch the TV in silence for a while. Sera holds his hand.

                              BEN
I like it here with you.

                              SERA
Let's stay for a while.

                              BEN
OK.
    CUT TO:

107 INT. MOTEL ROOM. DAY

Ben mixes a cocktail for himself, then one for Sera. The camera follows him as he goes . . .

108 EXT. POOL-SIDE. DAY

. . . to the side of the pool, where Sera is sunbathing. He lowers himself unsteadily into the chair but avoids spilling a drop of the drinks, which he puts down on to a glass-topped table. He is pretty loaded. Sera turns over and moves out of his shadow.

                              SERA
I've missed the best sun. Why did you have to pawn your watch?

I didn't know I'd ever need it again.

Sera gets up, takes a drink and then walks to the diving board. As she takes a position at the end, she pulls the bathing suit out from her bottom, does a very natural dive into the pool, swims a length under water and then comes out near Ben, pulls herself out of the pool in one move and bends down and kisses Ben for a long time. Ben responds and kisses her back. There is no one else around the pool.

The kiss becomes heated and urgent and Sera sits on Ben, making him wet from her. He pushes the top of her suit down and kisses her breasts. She picks up the glass and drinks, letting the alcohol spill from her mouth, over her breasts. Ben drinks from her.

Take this off.

He tries to pull her swimsuit down.

SERA

Maybe we should go inside. Come on.

She stands up, covering herself. Ben stands up, laughing, loses his balance and slips on the wet concrete. He falls backwards, half on to the chair, which breaks, and then on to the glass table. The table goes over and it and the glasses all shatter on the concrete. Ben falls on to the broken glass and cuts himself all over his back and his arms. Glass goes into the pool. Blood mingles with the water on the steaming cement.

BEN

Whoops.

Sera picks up her towel and lays it down next to him. She kneels and helps him up, trying to pull out the little bits of glass sticking to him. Ben stands unsteadily.

I'll go and clean up. Perhaps you could take care of this.

He indicates the mess, then walks to their room. Sera begins carefully picking up the broken glass. The desk clerk appears with a broom and a dustpan.

DESK-CLERK
(*cheerfully*)

Everybody OK?

SERA

Yes, fine. Don't worry. We'll pay for the chair, and I'll clean all
this up, the pool too.

DESK-CLERK

Don't worry.

*He begins sweeping the broken glass into the pan, cheerfully ignoring
Sera.*

SERA

You seem prepared for accidents.

DESK-CLERK
(*still smiling*)

Yeah . . . we get a lot of screw-ups here.

He looks directly at Sera.

Now, you two keep your loud talk and your liquor to your room.
Check out first thing tomorrow and after that I don't want to see

either of you here again. I don't need you paying for the chair or cutting your pretty hands on the glass. Let's leave it at that.

Nodding firmly, he goes back to the mess, indicating that the conversation is over.

See ya in the morning.

CUT TO:

109 INT. MOTEL ROOM. DAY

Sera comes into the room.

                              SERA

Ben?

She sees that he is already asleep on the bed, his half-naked body covered with countless bits of bloodstained tissue. The image has an almost religious feel to it. The TV is on and a sitcom is playing.

Something funny catches Sera's attention. She laughs and sits on the bed next to Ben.

                    (*voice-over*)

I think we realized that we didn't have long and accepted it. My charm, for him, was that I accepted him exactly as he was and didn't expect him to change. I think we both realized that about each other. Ben needed me and I liked his drama. I loved him.

CUT TO:

110 EXT. DESERT LANDSCAPE. DUSK

We see Las Vegas lighting up. The blue rental car passes through frame and drives towards the town.

FADE OUT:

FADE UP ON:

111 INT. SERA'S BEDROOM. LAS VEGAS. NIGHT

Ben wakes from a dream. He is fully clothed and very agitated.

                              BEN

Sera?

89

112 INT. KITCHEN. NIGHT

Sera is cooking.

SERA

I'm in here. You probably don't want to hear about it right now, but I bought some plain rice. I thought it might be something you could eat. So if you get hungry later on, just let me know.

Ben comes in from the kitchen and takes vodka bottles from the fridge.

113 SCENE CUT.

114 SCENE CUT.

115 INT. BATHROOM. NIGHT

Ben's hands are sweating and it is difficult for him to keep hold of the bottle as he drinks. He gets most of it down and then he hunches over the sink and immediately vomits. He takes the second bottle and tries again.
   CUT TO:

116 INT. SHOWER. NIGHT

Still holding the bottle, Ben stands in the shower. He drinks some more and closes his eyes.
   CUT TO:

117 INT. KITCHEN. NIGHT

Ben enters, smartly dressed and smiling.

BEN

I think I'm ready for the rice!
   CUT TO:

118 INT. DINING ROOM. LATER THAT NIGHT

Ben and Sera sitting opposite each other. He has a bowl of rice, which he is pretending to eat in between sips of vodka. She has a bowl of vegetables and rice. She sits, silently for a while, and then puts down her chopsticks.

SERA

You're pretty sick.

Ben looks away.

What are you going to do?

She folds her arms.

I want you to go see a doctor.

He thinks for a while and then turns to meet her gaze. They look right into each other's eyes.

BEN

Sera . . . I'm not going to see a doctor.

Sera continues to look at him almost defiantly.

Maybe it's time I moved to a hotel.

SERA

And do what . . . rot away in a room?
(*becoming angry*)
We're not going to talk about that. Fuck you! I will not talk about that. You're staying here. You are not moving to a hotel.

BEN

Will you lighten up, please?

SERA
(*close to tears*)
One thing . . . one thing . . . this is one thing you can do for me. I've given you gallons of free will here! You can do this for me.

She leans right forward.

Let's face it. Sick as you are, I'm probably the only thing that's keeping you alive.

She stands up.

I have to go to work now.

Ben doesn't say anything. He just stares a hole in his bowl of rice.
CUT TO:

91

Ben walks by himself. He is deep in thought.
    CUT TO:

120 INT. CASINO. NIGHT

Ben recklessly bets two hundred dollars at the craps table . . . and wins.
As he leans forward to collect his winnings, he sees . . .
    ANGLE:

. . . a Blonde in a very low-cut outfit. She smiles at Ben and walks
around the table to pick him up. Ben puts all of his winnings on one bet
and wins again. This pattern repeats a few times and drinks are on the
house.

                        BLONDE
Hey . . . that was quite a play. You in for the convention?

    Ben gets to the point.

                        BEN
I'd like to fuck you.

    A few people hear Ben and the Blonde is almost put off, but he does

92

have about eight thousand dollars in winnings and so she leans in very close so that she can talk quietly.

                              BLONDE
I'm very expensive.

                              BEN
How mush to lick your pussy?

The Blonde picks up a sizeable stack of chips and looks at Ben.
CUT TO:

121 INT. SERA'S HOUSE. LATER THAT NIGHT

Sera lets herself in, looks around and opens the bedroom door.
ANGLE:

In one fluid movement the naked blonde gets off the semi-conscious Ben, pulls her dress over her head and walks past Sera. Moments later we hear the front door slam. Ben comes to and looks at Sera. He is more or less unaware of what has just happened.

                              BEN
Hello . . .
ANGLE ON SERA

Her eyes are wet.

                              SERA
There are limits.

                              BEN
                          (remembering)
Yes . . . I guess I knew that.

Ben gets out of the bed. He picks up the bottle on the bedside table and stands.

Perhaps I could crash on the couch for a few hours . . . and then I'll leave.

He walks out of the room and closes the door. Camera moves in on Sera. She covers her face with her hands. She drops her purse and slides down the wall to the floor, weeping quietly.

SERA
(*voice-over*)

I heard the door slam a couple of hours later and he was gone.

FADE OUT:

FADE IN:

122 EXT. STREET. DAY

Ben coming out of a liquor store with a large brown bag.

CUT TO:

123 EXT. STREET. NIGHT

Sera getting out of a car. The car drives off. Sera examines her face in a pocket mirror. Puts on more lipstick.

CUT TO:

124 INT. MOTEL ROOM. DAY

Ben is on all fours in the bathroom trying to vomit. His thin frame is heaving. Bottles are everywhere.

CUT TO:

125 EXT. THE STRIP. NIGHT

Three college boys with beer bottles walk The Strip. They are all wearing the same numbered jersey. Nice middle-class boys looking for an adventure. They see Sera and go into a huddle before walking over to her.

TALLEST COLLEGE BOY

How much will it cost us to fuck you?

The other two College Boys titter. Sera starts to walk away and then hesitates.

SERA

Sorry, guys, but I don't know what you mean. Anyway, I never date more than one guy at a time.

SMALLEST COLLEGE BOY

Come on . . . we got money . . . show her the money.

*The other College Boy gets out his wallet and opens it to show her.
Sera hesitates, not somehow comfortable with the situation, then goes
ahead.*

                              SERA
How much of that money did you guys want to spend?

                      TALLEST COLLEGE BOY
How much you want? How about two hundred for an hour?

                              SERA
                    (*becoming annoyed with them*)
Don't your friends talk?
                          (*no answer*)
Try three-hundred for a half-hour.

                      OTHER COLLEGE BOY
                          (*nervous*)
Three hundred for the hour.

                              SERA
OK . . . three . . . and we'll see how it goes. Where are you
staying?

                      TALLEST COLLEGE BOY
The Yukon, room twenty-four.

                              SERA
I'll see you there in fifteen minutes. You can pay me then. Why
don't you all take a shower while you're waiting.

                      OTHER COLLEGE BOY
A shower? In fifteen minutes?

                              SERA
Look . . . I'll only need one of you at a time. RIGHT?
UNDERSTOOD? So . . . the other two can shower while I'm
there. OK?

   They walk off in a huddle, giggling – three small boys.
   CUT TO:

126 EXT. YUKON MOTEL. NIGHT

Sera drinks from a beer bottle as she approaches their room. She talks to herself.

> SERA
>
> Where are the boys this weekend, Frank? Why, hell, Charlie, I sent 'em off to learn the one thing I couldn't teach 'em.

She looks at the numbers and finds the room. She knocks and a moment later the Tallest College Boy opens the door in his jockey shorts.

127 INT. MOTEL ROOM. NIGHT

Sera steps in. One boy is coming out of the bathroom wearing a towel and the third is sitting in a chair smoking a cigarette, which he passes to the boy in the towel. The other boy is fooling around with a video camera. The atmosphere is weird and Sera is suddenly alert.

The Tallest College Boy hands her the money. He is very well built, a football player. Sera hesitates, holding the money. The Tallest College Boy closes the door and then leans against it. They are all staring at her now. No one says anything. Sera smiles suddenly and puts the money in her purse. All business.

> SERA
>
> OK . . . where's the bedroom, and who's first?

They all look at each other.

> SMALLEST COLLEGE BOY
>
> I want to fuck her in the butt . . .

He looks at the other.

. . . you too, right?

> SERA
>
> Forget that. No one's doing that. You'll all go one at a time. If you want I'll suck you instead, but that's all. Then I'm out of here.

> SMALLEST COLLEGE BOY
> *(looking at tallest)*
>
> You said I could fuck her in the butt.

Shut up.

SMALLEST COLLEGE BOY
(*shouting*)
It's my fucking money.

SERA
That's it . . . Take your money back. I'm leaving.

The Smallest College Boy gets off the bed and comes over to Sera.

SMALLEST COLLEGE BOY
No . . . don't go.

The Tallest College Boy is still standing in front of the door and things are getting strange. The Other Boy turns on the video camera. Sera loses her cool.

SERA
(*to the Smallest College Boy*)
Maybe you'd like to fuck one of your friends in the butt instead.

The room goes very quiet. The kid tears up. Sera tries to back-pedal.

Hey . . . I'm sorry . . .

The kid punches her hard in the stomach, knocking her to the ground.
CUT TO BLACK:

QUICK FADE IN:

Close-up on Sera's face pushed into a bloodstained pillow, her body being pounded from behind. The naked legs of two of the boys behind her. We hear voices, filtered, from a long way off.

VOICE
Go on . . . fuck her ass . . .

OTHER VOICE
Look at me . . . look at me . . . look at me.

A hand comes into frame and pulls her head up by the hair. A pair of legs moves in. There is the sound of a punch.
FADE OUT:

FADE IN:

Sera's body on the floor. In the background trousers being hastily pulled on to legs. The boys exit with sport bags.

The last one turns out the lights and closes the door.
FADE OUT:

FADE IN:

128 INT. MOTEL ROOM. DAWN

In the half-light Sera gets up and walks with difficulty to the bathroom.

129 INT. BATHROOM. DAWN

She clicks on the mirror light. Her face is awful. One eye is swollen almost shut. Her top lip is cut.
  CUT TO BLACK:

130 INT. CAB. EARLY MORNING

Sera gets into the cab with considerable difficulty. The cab driver is a cynic.

                    CAB DRIVER
What's the matter, honey, get a back-door delivery you weren't expecting? You gonna be able to pay the fare?

  Without speaking she takes out a twenty, leans forward and drops it on the front passenger seat. He drives. Looks at her in the mirror.

Oh, don't wanna talk to me, unh? Well, don't take it out on me, I'm just covering my ass. What the hell do you expect, sluttin' around like that . . . dressed like that? You oughta be glad the creep didn't nail ya.
  CUT TO:

131 EXT. SERA'S HOUSE. MORNING

As the cab drives off, Sera walks slowly to the door.

Here Landlord's Wife passes and takes in her face.
  CUT TO:

99

132 INT. SERA'S SHOWER. DAY

Sera is slumped on the floor of the shower, her arms hugging her legs, the water pounding down on her.
    CUT TO:

133 INT. SERA'S HOUSE. DAY

Sera opens the door and we see the Landlord. Behind him, on the sidewalk, we can see his Wife. He is embarrassed.
    ANGLE

Sera, wearing dark glasses. She looks terrible. Her mouth is swollen and some of the bruising around her eye is visible.

LANDLADY

I'm sorry . . . but we'd like you out by the end of the week.
    CUT TO:

134 EXT. WHOLE YEAR INN. DAY

Sera gets out of a cab and goes into reception. She is wearing huge dark glasses to hide the black eye and the bruising.
    CUT TO:

135 INT. HOTEL. DAY

The desk clerk is wearing a shirt of Ben's that we recognize from an earlier scene.

DESK CLERK

I'm sorry, ma'am. He never checked back in.
    CUT TO:

136 EXT. THE STRIP. NIGHT

Sera walks alone. She's dejected as she looks for Ben.

137 INT. CASINO. NIGHT

Sera comes to an elevator and waits. She is wearing a thin black top without a bra. Her bruised face makes her suddenly very conspicuous and vulnerable. A big man in a white stetson stands next to her. He looks at

101

her and grins. She smiles, coldly. He takes from his pocket two black, hundred dollar chips, places one in each hand and deliberately places each one against her nipples. Other people see this and stop and watch. Sera looks down at his hands and stares until the man becomes uncomfortable.

STETSON MAN

What's the problem, honey? . . . You on strike?

And he walks away laughing.
CUT TO:

138 EXT. 7-ELEVEN. DAY

Sera is sitting on a freshly-painted red kerb. She smokes a cigarette and doesn't give a damn that her short skirt is somewhat revealing. Opposite her a bum is sleeping on the pavement. For a moment it looks like Ben. The camera comes in tight on to her face. She looks more lost that we've ever seen her. She drinks coffee from a styrofoam cup. The sun is bright and hot and traffic is noisy.

139 INT. DOCTOR'S OFFICE. DAY
Improvised scene.*

140 INT. CASINO. NIGHT

Sera comes in and the camera follows her as she makes her way to the bar. She has covered up much of the bruising with make-up but it is still pretty obvious. In wide shot we see her strike up a conversation with the man next to her at the bar.
CLOSE SHOT – THE BAR

A hand comes into shot and grips her arm firmly. We see that it is a casino security guard.

SERA

Let go. What's the problem.

SECURITY GUARD

We don't want you in here, that's the problem. Let's go.

And he jerks her arm. People are watching now.

*See Afterword.

102

> SERA

Don't worry . . . If you don't want me in here, then I don't want to be in here. Just let go of my arm and I'll walk out of here.

> SECURITY GUARD

Yeah . . . we'll both walk out now.

He steers her firmly across the floor.
CUT TO:

141 EXT. CASINO. NIGHT

They reach the sidewalk and, without relaxing his grip, he grabs her between the legs with his free hand and says in her ear:

> SECURITY GUARD

Next time it won't be so fucking easy.

And he pushes her towards the street and walks back into the Casino. Sera is shocked. She looks around and the group of people who have stopped to watch the event move away.

142 INT. SERA'S HOUSE. DAY

Sera is throwing clothes into a suitcase. The phone rings. She thinks about it for a long time and then it stops. She carries on packing and then the phone rings again. She picks it up.

> SERA

Hello . . . hello . . .
> *(suddenly alert)*

Ben? Where the fuck are you? Give me the address.
CUT TO:

143 INT. CAB. LATE AFTERNOON

The driver is black and friendly. The radio drones quietly – a religious programme. The Rev. Ike is taking listeners' calls.

> BLACK DRIVER

What in hell happened to you, Miss?

> SERA

Oh . . . it was an argument.

BLACK DRIVER

Leave him, Miss. Pretty girl like you could get any man that you
wanted.

144 INT. BEN'S MOTEL ROOM. DUSK

*The door opens. Ben is naked. His body looks bad. Leaving the door
open, he retreats to the bed.*

145 INT. BEN'S MOTEL ROOM. NIGHT

*Sera comes in, closing the door behind her. The shades are drawn and
the room is gloomy. Ben has got back into bed. She comes to the bed
and sits.*

SERA

Ben . . . I've been looking for you. Have you been here since you
left? It smells bad in here. It's so dark.

She clicks on the bedside light and is truly shocked by his face.

BEN

I wanted to see you . . .

SERA

Oh, Ben . . . you look so very sick . . . my love . . . you're so pale.

*She goes to the bathroom and returns with a wet face-cloth. She wipes
his face.*

BEN

I wanted to see you . . . you're my angel.

*He sits up painfully and finds a bottle, summoning up some last
strength to drink. His entire body shudders as he drains the bottle. He
puts it down and focuses on her for the first time. He sees her
damaged face, touches her face, looks at her questioningly.*

SERA

Something went wrong . . . I'm OK.

Ben begins to cry and that sets her off.

BEN

I'm sorry I put us assunder.

104

She shakes her head, unable to speak for the moment. She gets into bed with him, kissing his face. She caresses his whole body, which is shaking, possessed by an uncontrollable fever.

See how hard you make me, angel.

She excites him with her hand, kissing his face gently. When he is about to come, she straddles him and brings him inside. As he comes, he opens his eyes wide and looks at her.

You know I love you . . . yeah?

                        SERA
                    (*she comes*)
Yes.
SLOW FADE TO BLACK:

FADE IN:

Sera is sleeping. A sudden gasp wakes her. Ben is having a spasm. Suddenly his body relaxes. He turns his head, opens his eyes wide and looks straight at her.

                        BEN
Oh . . . I'm so sorry . . .

He smiles and turns his head away. He is very still.

                        SERA
Ben . . . Ben . . . Ben?
CUT TO:

146 INT. BEN'S MOTEL ROOM. NIGHT

In the darkened room we can just make out Sera sitting on the bed, looking at the still form of Ben.
CUT TO:

147 EXT. STREET NEAR MOTEL. DAWN

Sera walking. A paramedic van goes past with its lights flashing. The soundtrack is empty – silent. We slowly fade in theme music and titles start to roll.

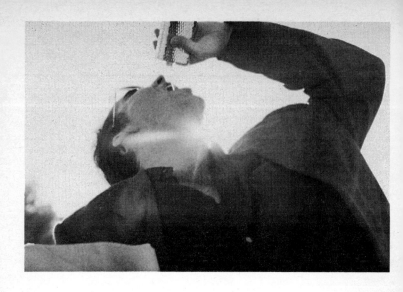

PUBLISHER'S NOTE

This text is based on the shooting script of September 1994, which was redefined substantially in the editing process (see Afterword).

CREDITS

College Boy #1	MICHAEL GOORJIAN
College Boy #2	JEREMY JORDAN
College Boy #3	DAVID LEE WILLSON
Cynical Cabbie	XANDER BERKELEY
Stetson Man at Casino	SERGIO PREMOLI
Security Guard	GORDON MICHAELS
Concerned Cabbie	LOU RAWLS
Stunt Coordinator	RUSSELL TOWERY
Stunt Players	DIANE TOWERY
	BRUCE BARBOUR
	JEFF SMOLEK
	DICK HANCOCK
Directed by	MIKE FIGGIS
Produced by	LILA CAZES AND
	ANNIE STEWART
Screenplay by	MIKE FIGGIS
Based upon the novel by	JOHN O'BRIEN
Executive Producers	PAIGE SIMPSON AND
	STUART REGEN
Director of Photography	DECLAN QUINN
Production Designer	WALDEMAR KALINOWSKI
Edited by	JOHN SMITH
Music by	MIKE FIGGIS
Costume Designer	LAURA GOLDSMITH
Casting by	CARRIE FRAZIER
Line Producer/	
Unit Production Manager	MARC S. FISCHER
1st Assistant Director	GARY MARCUS
2nd Assistant Director	SIMONE FAREER
Art Director	BARRY M. KINGSTON
Set Decorator	FLORENCE FELLMAN
Leadman	RUSS ANDERSON
On-Set Dresser	AMY H. ABRAMS
Swing Gang	STEPHEN PFAUTER
	JASON JOHN HADLEY
	GHISLAIN MANDON
Art Department Coordinator	REBECCA YOUNG
Camera Operator	MARIE PENDERSON
1st Assistant Camera	STEPHEN PIZZO
1st Assistant B-Camera	BONNIE BLAKE

Loader	BERNADETTE ECHO HAWK
Still Photographer	SUZANNE HANOVER
Assembly Editor	JINX GODFREY
Assistant Editors	ANNETTE WILLIAMS
	PAUL KNIGHT
Sound Mixer	PAWEL WDOWCZAK
Property Master	ZEEV TANKUS
Assistant Property Master	ANNE MARI ZIECKER
Script Supervisor	JANEE HULL-PAGE
Gaffer	TOBY IRWIN
Best Boy Electric	PAUL R. BIRK
Electricians	TODD HEATER
	FLINT ELLSWORTH
	JAMES DAVIS
	SEAN MARK MCKELVEY
Key Grip	KEVIN SMYTH
Best Boy Grip	RICK BOYLE
Dolly Grip	CHRISTIAN E. DIRKES
Grips	JOHN JOSEPH MINARDI
	T. J. TOLLEFSON
Costume Supervisor	LEESA EVANS
Set Costumer	VICKIE BRINKKORD
Assistant Costumers	JEAN DAVIS
Ms Shue's Wardrobe Features Outfits by	
VIVIENNE WESTWOOD	
Key Make-up Artist	KATY BIHR
Key Hair Stylist	BEATRICE DeALBA
Make-up Artist/Hair Stylist	LINDA HARDY
Location Manager	DAVID HALDIMAN
Assistant Location Manager	CRAIG W. VAN GUNDY
Production Supervisor	ROBIN L. GREEN
Assistant Production Coordinator	JAMES A. CAPP
Clearances	MARK MORGAN
Post Production Supervisor	MICHAEL SAXTON
Post Production Coordinator	DANA PADGETT
Special Effects Supervisor	WILLIAM HARRISON
Effectsmen	MATHEW POPE
	ALBERT MARANGONI
Special Effects Services Provided by	SPECIAL EFFECTS UNLIMITED, INC.
Construction Coordinator	CHUCK PHILLIPS
Construction Foreman	CHARLES PAGE
Assistant to Mr Figgis	AMANDA BLUE

Assistant to Mr Cage	L. M. SOBLE
	JEFF LEVINE
Set Production Assistants	MARK ANTHONY LITTLE
	T. KEVIN BEARD
	ROMANY TURNER
	GEOFFREY TEAGARDIN
	EDDIE PICKET
	TY PENNINGTON
Office Production Assistant	SHANNON E. REILLY
Construction PA/Driver	SETH PHILLIPS
Production Accountant	HARVE K. MALKIN
Assistant Production Accountant	CARL MASTROMARINO
Unit Publicist	LEONARD MORPURGO
Stand-In for Mr Cage	MARCO KYRIS
Stand-In for Ms Shue	MARTEE LA COMETTE
Casting Associate	STACEY ROSEN
Transportation Coordinator	DEREK RASER
Transportation Captain	J. T. THAYER
Drivers	SCOTT GOUDREAU
	STEVE EARLE
	JENNIFER BLUM
	KATHY L. MACMILLAN
	DON FEENEY
	TRACY THIELEN
	EARL THIELEN
	MARK WILLIS
Insert Car Driver	BRIAN KAHN
Mr Cage's Driver	TODD ROWLAND
Catering	THE ARRANGEMENT
Las Vegas Catering	SIGNATURE CATERERS
Craft Service	PETER EVANGELATOS
Laughlin/Las Vegas Craft Service	VALERIE BURNLEY
Video Playback	STEVE IRWIN
Interlock Projection	BACKGROUND ENGINEERING
Lead Scenic	MICHAEL BLAICH
Carpenter	BOB HAWK
Supervising Sound Editor	NIGEL HEATH
Dialogue Editor	MATHEW KNIGHTS
Effects Editor	JULIAN SLATER
Assistant Sound Editor	JAMES FELTHAM
Sound Rerecorded at	MAGMASTERS LIMITED
Foley Editor	ROD HOWICK

Foley Artists	JASON SWANSCOTT
	ANDIE DERRICK
Dubbing Mixer	HENRY DOBSON
Assistant Dubbing Mixer	DANNY SHEEHAN
Negative Cutter	TRU CUT LONDON
Color Timer	COLIN COULL
	METROCOLOR LONDON LTD.
Post-Production Laboratory	METROCOLOR LONDON LTD.
'The Making Of' Documentary Team	RICHARD DAVENPORT
	ROMANY TURNER
	AMANDA BLUE
Payroll Services	AXIUM PAYROLL SERVICES
Legal Services	ARMSTRONG HIRSCH JACKOWAY
	TYERMAN & WERTHEIMER
	GEORGE T. HAYUM, ESQ.
Completion Bond Provided by	FILM FINANCES
	ADAM MOCS
Insurance by	GREAT NORTHERN/REIFF &
	ASSOCIATES
Post Production Accounting	RC BARAL & CO., INC.
Paintings in LA Bank by	JAMES SCOTT
Paintings in Sera's Apartment by	ANN MARI OLLSSON
Artwork by	RODRIGO PIMENTEL
	GUSTAVO RAMOS RIVERA
	FLORENCIO GELABERT
	Courtesy of ITURRALDE GALLERY

'THE THIRD MAN'
Courtesy of LUMIERE PICTURES LIMITED

Original Score Composed by	MIKE FIGGIS
Featured Vocalist	STING
Featured Musicians	DAVE HARTLEY (Piano)
	CHRIS LAURENCE (Double Bass)
	TONY COE (Tenor Saxophone/Clarinet)
	IAN THOMAS (Drums)
	MAGGIE NICOLS (Vocalist)
	ED DEANE (Electric Guitar)
	RAY WARLEIGH (Alto Saxophone)
	MIKE FIGGIS (Trumpet/Keyboards)

'ANGEL EYES'
Written by Matt Dennis and Earl Brent
Performed by Sting

III

Courtesy of A&M Records, Inc.

'IT'S A LONESOME OLD TOWN'
Written by Harry Tobias and Charles Kisco
Performed by Sting
Courtesy of A&M Records, Inc.

'MY ONE AND ONLY LOVE'
Written by Robert Mellin and Guy Wood
Performed by Sting
Courtesy of A&M Records, Inc.

'LONELY TEARDROPS'
Written by Berry Gordy, Gwen Gordy-Fuqua and Billy Davis
Performed by Michael McDonald
Courtesy of Giant Records
By Arrangement with Warner Special Products

'COME RAIN OR COME SHINE'
Written by Johnny Mercer & Harold Arlen
Performed by Don Henley
Courtesy of Geffen Records

'RIDICULOUS'
Written by Nicolas Cage & Phil Roy
Performed by Nicolas Cage

'I WON'T BE GOING SOUTH (FOR A WHILE)'
Written by Angelo Paladino
Performed by The Paladinos
Courtesy of Pangaea Records

'THE THIRD MAN THEME'
Written by Anton Karas

'YOU TURN ME ON'
Written by Jacques Morali and Alain Bernardin
Courtesy of The Crazy Horse Saloon, Paris

SOUNDTRACK AVAILABLE ON PANGAEA RECORDS
RELEASED THROUGH I.R.S. RECORDS

Music Supervisor	GEMMA DEMPSEY
Original Score Engineer	AUSTIN INCE
Musician's Contractor	ISOBEL GRIFFITHS
Music Clearance	CLEARANCE CONSULTANTS

Special Thanks:
THE O'BRIEN FAMILY
EVERYONE AT THE WHITEHOUSE – London
RANDOLPH PITTS
CLAUDIA BUCHANAN
BRIGID BUCKMAN
LOIS KAY
COCA COLA, USA
CARILLON IMPORTERS, LTD.
GOLD RIVER CASINO AND RESORT – Laughlin, Nevada
COCK & BULL PUB – Santa Monica, California
COMPUTER FILM COMPANY – London
NEIL AT MIDNIGHT TRANSFER – London
CECILIA SKJORTEN
ELAINE DAVIS
HOLLY SIMPSON
TONY DINGMAN
BIENCHEN & LOUIS
STING
MILES COPELAND
LAKE HOUSE STUDIOS
ARLEN FIGGIS
ANTHONY MARINELLI
SIMON OSBORNE – ENGINEER
SNAKE RANCH STUDIOS – London
RED MULLET STUDIO – Barnet

Filmed with PANAVISION Aaton cameras and lenses
Camera cranes and dollies by CHAPMAN
Color by FOTO-KEM FOTO-TRONICS
Titles and Opticals by CINE IMAGE FILM OPTICALS LTD
Edited on Avid technology at THE WHITEHOUSE, London
No. 33977 MPAA
© 1995 Initial Productions
All Right Reserves
Distributed by MGM/UA DISTRIBUTION CO. (US)
and by ENTERTAINMENT (UK)
Running time: approximately 112 minutes

1 Mike Figgis with Nicholas Cage and Elisabeth Shue

2 Mike Figgis with Julian Sands

3 Mike Figgis with Bob Rafelson

4 Mike Figgis with Laurie Metcalf; Nicholas Cage and
Elisabeth Shue in the background

AFTERWORD

I thought it might be interesting to talk about how the film redefined itself in the editing room. The Editor was John Smith and this is his first feature. I met John because he had cut the five commercials that I have shot. I like his work and asked him one day if he had ever considered cutting a feature. It seemed no one had ever asked him. So I did. He came to the film with none of the preconceptions or rules that pervade feature editing and he was prepared to try anything. We've also worked together on art documentaries on Vivienne Westwood and William Forsythe, the American choreographer who heads the Frankfurt Ballet.

FINAL CUT SEQUENCE

Note: first number denotes position of scene in completed film; the number in square brackets denotes position of scene in the original shooting script.

1 [56]   Ben in a liquor store filling a trolley and whistling. Originally designed for a much later sequence. We dropped it altogether from the film and then, quite late in the day, I put it back in as the opening shot because it so clearly states something about Ben's character.

2 [1]   Ben comes into smart LA restaurant and bums some money from his ex agent.
This is the first time Nic improvised the expression 'outstanding', which is the trade mark of a well-known agent in LA. The two actors playing the agents, Steven Weber and Richard Lewis, based their performances on other well-known agents.

3 [26]   Ben in an LA bar drinking heavily. Tries to pick up Teri (Valeria Golino).
We got into a bit of trouble here because Nic (with my approval) sang a song called 'You Turn Me On'. He'd heard this in a famous strip club in Paris and recorded it on a voice recorder. When it came to clearing the song in post-production, the club

refused to let us use it. The writer of the song was dead, the owner of the club was dead and the estate was in litigation. Up until the last minute it seemed as if we were going to have to take it out and I had no cover at all. And then they relented.

One of the shots of the barman in this scene is completely out of focus but the bottles behind him are sharp, so I felt OK about using the shot because I could rationalize to myself that it was a drunk's POV. I think we went through three focus pullers on the shoot.

4 [*13, 27*]   Ben, drinking and driving, is buzzed by a cop on a motorbike.

5 [*28*]   Ben in a strip club. Drinks bottle of Scotch.
This was supposed to be a much longer scene with dialogue but it was too slow and literal. The dancer was very beautiful and had a slightly eerie quality. We found her in a trendy strip club in LA. Nic took Lisa Shue and I out on the town in the rehearsal period. We set off in a Bentley with a driver, drank expensive Scotch and listened to 'Kind of Blue' by Miles Davis. We arrived at the club which was full of agents and producers having bachelor parties. Lots of blondes with huge breasts paraded on the stage and it became clear that the gig involved choosing a girl who would then dance exclusively for her patron of the moment. One of the girls was stunning and I made the mistake of saying this aloud. Minutes later she approached our table, introduced herself to me (we actually shook hands), and began dancing. The next day I asked the production office to call her and offer her the job.

The older man who Ben sits next to in the strip club is the actor Al Henderson. I used him on *Mr Jones*. He plays a sound mixer in the film *Modern Romance* and has the line. 'You saved the movie.'

I tried something new here. When Ben drinks the bottle of Scotch and then goes into shock, I pull out the sound, everything – the music, the atmos, the effects. I have always wanted to do it but in the past have been talked out of it by engineers and mixers who told me that something has to be left on the track, even if it is only white noise. I enjoy watching this sequence with an audience because it does have an unnerving effect. The cinema goes quiet, a rare thing. When the sound comes back Ben's voice is distanced but the music is not and it is not until he crosses the street in traffic that things come back to normal.

6 [*31*]   Ben picks up a young prostitute on Sunset.

7 [*32, 34, 36*]   Ben and prostitute behind motel on Sunset.
Ben's one line here is as much back-story as we need: 'Can't
remember if I started drinking because my wife left me . . . or my
wife left me because I started drinking, but fuckitanyway.'

8 [*33, 35, 37, 39*]   Ben wakes up on his kitchen floor.
I am very happy with the sound on the film. I went back to a style
of mixing that has always interested me. For example, in this scene
as Ben wakes we hear the sound of the refrigerator. Then we hear
the sound of his watch as he brings his hand to his face. As the
prostitute takes his ring there is the sound of teeth on metal and a
distant siren. Never do we hear Ben's breathing, or the movement
of his clothes.

9 [*38*]   Flashback to prostitute stealing his ring.

10 [*40*]   Ben goes to the bank but is shaking too much to sign the
back of the cheque.

11 [*41*]   Ben has a drink in a bar. Barman ticks him off for being a
drunk.
There was no coverage on this scene because we were in such a
hurry that I decided to risk it and shoot the complete scene in one
take. This means that it is very difficult to shorten the performance
in the editing. The barman is played by Graham Beckel, a fine
actor with whom I worked on *Liebestraum*. Our claim to fame on
that film was that he performed the longest screen piss of all time.

12 [*42*]   Ben back at the bank. Recites erotic poem and signs his
cheque.
One of the scenes that I cut (Scene 10) involved a drunken fantasy
of Ben's in which he is in the bar and a game show is playing on
the TV. Carry Lowel, the actress who plays the bank teller also
played the part of the game show hostess. I liked the scene very
much because it reminded me of a section of one of my favourite
books of all time, *A Fan's Notes* by Frederick Exley. In Exley's
book his hero has a fantasy that a soap becomes more than real
and all the characters start talking dirty and fornicating. Alas, my
game show sequence slowed the narrative down and it had to hit
the floor.

13 [*11*]   Ben at work faking phone calls, faking deals.

In John O'Brien's book, on which the script is based, it was never made clear what Ben did for a living. It was my idea to make him a film person. People have asked me to define his job but I cannot. Like so many people making a handsome living in what is known as Hollywood, Ben has an office, several hundred scripts and makes phone calls in which as many names are dropped as possible. But I still don't know what Ben, or indeed they, do for a living. It was Nic's idea to hold the phone upside down.

The sympathetic woman who gives him his messages is played by the actress Susan Lange. I've known her for a long time. We first met at the La Mama Theater in New York and later at the Mickery Theatre in Amsterdam where we were both with performance art groups. She has been in most of my films. In *Liebestraum* she played dual roles of nurse and hooker. In *Mr Jones* she played a therapist. Even though this was a small part I raised the money to fly her in from New York.

14 [*12*]   Ben is fired by his boss, Bill, and given a cheque. Says he's moving to Vegas.

Bill is played by Tom Kopache. Kopache was in the same performance group as Susan Lange. He also performed in *Liebestraum* and *Mr Jones*, in which he gave an incredible performance as a mental patient. So convincing, that when the Tri-Star executives came to visit the set they steered well clear of him in the food line.

When I'd finished the first draft of the script I gave it to Bill Tennent to read. Bill is an ex-alcoholic. At one stage in his career he was one of the most successful of American agents but fell from grace and re-emerged five years later clean and sober. I met him when he was one of the producers on *Stormy Monday*, and we became friends. An active member of AA, Bill gave me some stiff advice about the morality of glamourizing drinking, which I took to heart and made changes (see Scene 55). There is something of Bill in the scene with Tom Kopache.

15 [*2, 3, 5, 6, 9*]   Title sequence intercut with Sera and Yuri in hotel suite with clients.

The first cut was fairly representational of the shooting script. But John Smith and I found that the story was too disjointed and it

119

was taking a very long time to get Ben out of LA and on his way to Vegas. I also found after the first cut that the real strength of the film lay in the relationship between Ben and Sera, and I wanted their relationship to start as soon as possible. So, we decided to try to create one long drinking session with Ben in LA and then get him out and on his way to Vegas. We changed the sequence around and it worked, although it did create a big continuity problem. Ben has his wedding ring stolen by the prostitute, but a couple of scenes later, as he is being fired, the ring is back on his finger because in the shooting script the scenes are the other way around. It would have been possible to go to a digital company and have the ring removed, but having shot on 16mm, and with very little money to play with, it seemed silly. Money did have to be spent on digital cleansing, though. In the title sequence a woman is seen doing a line of coke. Also in the shot was a bottle of vodka and we had to change the label because no booze company wants to be associated with the idea of alcoholism. (One very famous beer company offered us free booze *not* to put their label in the film.) So, we had to go into the image and redesign the label. It's an amazing process but costs thousands of dollars a second.

I made big cuts in the LA sequence, including most of the stuff with Ben and his house, the small boy next door, and Ben following a girl walking her dog and having thoughts about the colour of her underwear. They were all great scenes and I was sad to see them go, but in a sense they all repeated the idea that Ben is a poetic drunk. After a certain time they become tedious and self indulgent. With earlier films I would have found it difficult to lose such well acted scenes, but with this one it was a joy to find the rhythm by being this tough. Maybe they will find their way into the documentary that we shot at the same time.

The flying shots of Vegas by night were a late thought. When it became clear that we were not going to get the permissions to shoot much of the film in Vegas, I became concerned that we would not see enough of it and the film would start to feel low-budget – by which I mean there were too many interiors, etc. Marc Fischer, the Line Producer, agreed with me and we managed to scrape up enough money for three hours in a helicopter. It was exciting. At one point I asked the pilot (ex-Vietnam, of course) to do a tight circle around the glass pyramid of the Luxor Hotel. This pyramid has the most powerful light in the world coming out of its pinnacle and on a clear day it is visible to pilots in LA. I wanted a shot looking down into the light (like looking into hell). The pilot obliged and we went into the tightest of circles with cameraman Declan Quinn's eye glued to the camera monitor in the back and mine to the monitor in the front. Suddenly, the image span and I said: Wow, great move, sir.' He looked at me and said: 'Sorry, sometimes it's difficult to control those rising thermals coming off the desert.' The hot air had spun us around 360 degrees in a very short space of time. I used part of the shot, though, in Scene 79.

16 [54]   Sera talks to her shrink (#1).

                          SERA
You know, I bring out the best in the men who fuck me. I mean
. . . it's not easy, but I'm very good, I mean, it's amazing, it's
like . . . if I haven't worked for a really long time then . . .
boom, I can just turn on a dime. I can just be who they want me
to be. I walk into that room . . . and I know right away . . . this
is their fantasy and I become it. I'm that service, you know, I
just . . . I perform it and I perform it well. I mean, I'm an
equation most of the time. It's like thirty minutes of my body is
. . . costs $300 . . . well, that's just to get into the room and then
it's about $500 after that . . . you know . . . we negotiate but . . .
uhh . . . it's a performance, it's definitely a performance.

In pre-production I took a tough look at the script. This is always a crucial moment on a film because the actors are in place and practical decisions are being made about locations and so on. The story starts to be real. I liked the script but I had a nagging worry that Sera didn't have enough of a voice in the story. In the book there is a lot of internal thought from her, but in the script it was difficult to find a way of expressing those ideas. Her thoughts are about her job as well as about Ben and they are not the kind of ideas that could be expressed in the context of dialogue to him. Ben, on the other hand, is a drunk and has licence to be as expressive as he likes. For example, his thoughts in the bank are recorded on a portable tape machine and we learn something about him. Sera's character does not have that freedom. So I came up with with idea of her talking to a therapist (not a new device, I remember it in *Klute*). I went back to the book and found all the interesting stuff about her and put it into the script as therapy sessions. I reasoned that she would have plenty of cash and if everyone else in the US is talking to a shrink, why wouldn't a prostitute? Lila Cazes (the Producer from Lumière pictures) didn't like these changes at all and asked me to take them out of the script again, which I did. However, I was still concerned about the imbalance, so I did a sneaky thing. We shot a camera test the week before the shoot and I asked Elisabeth to wear her costume. I gave her all the deleted text to read and then, on camera, I interviewed her in her character as Sera and she improvised her answers based on the material from the book. Some other things came out of the sessions which had a lot more emotion in them, and I think these elements were crucial to her character. She told me afterwards that it was a great way of getting into character. I asked her about her life as a prostitute, about her feelings towards Ben when she first met him. Then she changed costume and we jumped forward in the script to where Ben has moved in with her, then we moved to the end and used the past tense as she talked about her feelings for him. A couple of days later I saw the results and was pleased. The Lumière folk were not happy that I'd done this, but I told them that it had cost them nothing and we should think of it as insurance and probably wouldn't use it. They calmed down, but in my heart I knew it would end up in the film.

Towards the end of the shoot I remembered the footage and thought I should take another look at it because, after all, on the day we did it Lisa hadn't even done a scene with Nic and hadn't really formed her character. I had in mind the idea of stealing an hour one night to do some more therapy. I asked Waldemar Kalinowsky (Production Designer) to get the couch ready. I viewed the footage again and was blown away by how accurate her emotions were. I was moved to tears by the last scene and cancelled the extra 'illegal' shoot.

None of these therapy scenes appeared in the first cut of the film. This was deliberate. I wanted to be absolutely sure that they were needed. Afterwards we quickly made a second pass and added everything. I particularly liked the speech about the fat hairy man. Interestingly enough, so did the American censors and they asked me to make significant cuts in this text for the US release. I'm beginning to realize the power of the word in film. Someone talking about sex is stronger than seeing sex. The same is true about death.

17 [*22, 24*]   Sera and Yuri have breakfast together.

18 [*20*]   Yuri and Sera in bed together.
The US censor asked for cuts here. They felt that Julian Sands's buttocks were too strong for the scene. Julian Sands is a great performer. This is the second of many films that I hope to make with him. I remember walking out of *Gothic* when it first came out, and then watching it again when I was making *The Browning Version* (sitting next to Julian). I loved it second time around. He is a great actor to work with, frightened of nothing. After the great LA earthquake, in the week of the two thousand tremors which followed the big one, Julian decided to inspect the foundations of his Hollywood house. To do this he had to inch his way around the crawl space at the bottom of the house. (Imagine potholing!) He's a man I'd choose to be in a trench with if a hostile army was advancing. (I think of film-making as trench warfare.)

19 [*43*]   Ben in the supermarket buying garbage bags and firelighters.

20 [*40, 45–8*]   Montage as Ben clears his house and burns personal things.

21 [*49–50*]   Montage as Ben drives to Vegas.
A couple of interesting stories about this sequence. When we were shooting the scenes in Ben's house, we ran out of time. We'd budgeted and scheduled a day for everything. Most of the day had been used up on all the scenes that later got cut from the film. Gary Marcus, the First AD, came to me and said that we had an hour left to shoot all of the scenes that involve Ben packing and clearing his house. After that our permit would run out and, as it was a residential area, we would be in trouble with the police if we carried on. In his opinion it was not possible to finish, so what did I want to do? It seemed that the only option was to come back, find some money from somewhere to pay for it (or sacrifice

another couple of scenes as a trade-off). This upset me because up until then we had stayed in budget and on schedule and with something as tight as this film I felt it was important to be on top.

Something else was bothering me. Things had slowed up. Because we were in a house for a whole day, equipment had started to appear and things were cluttering up the space; cable everywhere, lights everywhere, people everywhere making little camps of folding chairs and boxes and coffee cups. I hate all that stuff because I know equipment slows a film down and on this shoot I'd decreed that we'd have as little as possible. Nearly all the scenes were either hand-held or off a tripod.

I gathered everyone together and told them that we were going to finish the scenes in the remaining hour. I asked Declan if he could shoot on fast stock with available light and he said that he could. We cleared all the equipment out of the house and he put bright bulbs in all of the practical lights. The art department set up the props in all of the rooms. I talked to Nic and told him that we were going to shoot the whole sequence in one continuous take. He was delighted with the challenge. We put a radio mike on him so that we'd have a guide track in case he decided to speak or sing – this way we'd at least have a chance to replace the track in post-production. I quickly went over the route that he and Declan would have to take, discussed the pace and feel of the scene and then told them that from then on in they were on their own.

Within about twenty minutes the house was ready. Everyone except Nic, Declan and his assistant left the house and began packing up the trucks. I went out as well and had a cup of coffee and a cigarette, confident that great things were happening inside. This was confirmed a few days later when I saw the dailies. We finished on time and completed the day's shoot. I've never felt happier. The crew got away on time and the energy was still intact the next day because everybody felt that they had achieved something special. Despite the subject matter this was an immensely happy shoot.

The first cut of the film dealt with the journey to Vegas in real time. It was too slow and lacked urgency. Whilst reviewing the dailies on video at high speed I was struck by how much more interesting it looked at pace and asked John to consider cutting the whole sequence like that to the song 'Lonely Teardrops'. The

Michael MacDonald track had always been in my mind as a Ben song. It's that rare thing, a very sad song that has great energy and pace. I had some very scary moments trying to buy the rights and I'm very pissed off that it didn't end up on the album.

John went to work and when I saw his cut a few days later I was amazed. (I think there is a device like this in *After Hours*.) The film was cut on an Avid; a sequence like this would have been inconceivable on the traditional Steenbeck. On a computer you can see the finished effect straight away. Editing is going through its biggest revolution because of this new development.

22 [51]   Ben stops at the gas station and sees three Polish gangsters who discuss Yuri.
Waldemar Kalinowski has been my production designer on every film I've made in America. We hit it off when we met on *Internal Affairs* and quickly discovered we had many things in common. Waldemar trained as a rocket scientist in Poland, came to the US as a young man and worked as a photographer and an actor (*Heaven's Gate* and *Breathless*) before becoming a production designer. Rocket science had eluded me, but everything else was parallel. I thought it would be nice (and cheap) for us both to be Polish gangsters. On the first day of shooting I went off to the bathroom to slick down my hair and change, and when I came back on to the set I realized that the strange looks I was getting from the crew were because no one recognized me.

23 [52]   Ben arrives in Vegas at night.

24 [52A]   Ben almost runs Sera over.
As we were shooting this I decided to give then some dialogue. Something that would inform an audience that there was some kind of chemistry between them. I'm glad I did. This was also their first scene together.

25 [55]   Ben checks in at the 'Hole You're In' motel.

26 [57]   Sera and shrink (#2). Talks about the fat hairy man.

SERA
I walked into the room and he was lying on the bed. He had his arms behind his head. There was hair everywhere. He was really really fat and he had a large erection . . . I remember he was so

proud of his large erection.* And I asked him where my money was and he pointed at the dresser. And then I asked him what he wanted and he said, 'Lie down . . . I'm on top.' And he started pounding me really hard. I remember I had to bite my tongue to keep from crying. And then he did that for a while . . . and then I started to get up and he pushed me back down and he held my hair . . . he was pulling it and then he . . . stuck his penis in my mouth and it really hurt. So I tried to get up again and he said, 'Stay there, baby, I'm gonna come on your face.' So he did . . . and then he rubbed his semen all over my face and in my hair.* Then he kicked me off the bed and told me to leave.

27 [58–59]   Sera on the streets. Ben picks her up.
When we were editing this sequence I felt we needed a shot of her by herself on the street before she bumps into Ben. We didn't have one. Then I remembered that we'd shot a camera test with Lisa walking along Sunset. No one could find the shot or the negative. We searched and searched, to no avail. Eventually we gave up, but John Smith did find a video of the shot and we had that transferred to film. It has to be one of the darkest shots I've ever seen and if it wasn't for the fact that she's lighting a cigarette you wouldn't know anyone was there. But it does the trick. There's a lesson there.

28 [61, 64]   Ben and Sera go back to Ben's motel room. They don't have sex. She falls asleep.
US censors asked for cuts in this scene. They felt her head movements during the blow job were too realistic. It was difficult for us to recut the scene with as much power and I wasn't happy with the result. I'd argued that his singing here took away the perverse element of watching two people have sex. The singing came about because in the rehearsal Nic sang and, although I liked it, I was not about to get into a legal corner afterwards negotiating the rights to a song, as happened with 'You Turn Me On'. He then told me that he was the writer and that I could use it. I love the use of this song and I think it illustrates Cage's brilliance perfectly.

*The references to erect penis and coming on her face were deleted in the US release.

29   Road cleaning truck passes through frame. Sera wakes and exits.
It gave me great pleasure to use the road cleaning shot. It's a snip from a beautiful sequence that was designed to be the last shot in the film but got replaced because it was too dark.

30 [*65A*]   Sera hurries back to her house at dawn.
This was quite a late thought. I suddenly realized there were no 'establishing shots' of where she lives and, while I am not a fan of this kind of film-making, sometimes it is necessary to give the audience this kind of information. I was keen to show that she lives in a nice place and to get away from the clichés about prostitutes.

31 [*66*]   Yuri hits Sera for not earning enough money in the night.

32 [*8, 23*]   Flashback: Yuri cuts Sera with a knife.
Shot on slow colour film – pushed – printed as black and white. I've come to the conclusion that quite a lot of rubbish is talked about black and white. It's been my experience that the best results come from shooting on colour and then going to black and white. I think *Manhattan* was shot this way, but perhaps this is a myth.

33 [*21*]   Sera with shrink (#3). Talks about Yuri being paranoid.

SERA

Yeah . . . he cut me a couple of times. I mean . . . he'd always say, never on the face, so he cut me right here (indicates her bottom). He cried and I . . . I felt sorry for him. Well, in his mind I'd done something wrong but in my mind I . . . hadn't done anything bad. He's kind of paranoid.

34 [*68*]   Yuri on the streets of Vegas followed by Polish gangsters.

35 [*67*]   As Yuri tries to pawn his jewellery, Ben comes in and sells his Rolex Datona.
Dialogue was created on the spot. In the book they never meet but I love coincidences that go nowhere.

36 [*70*]   Sera fails to pick up a conventioneer. She is observed by another prostitute.
R. Lee Ermey, who plays the conventioneer was also the drill

sergeant in Kubrick's *Full Metal Jacket*. He came in for the evening to shoot this scene and we kept him waiting until about five in the morning, by which time everyone was punch drunk with fatigue. I felt bad about this. Mariska Hargitay, Jayne Mansfield's daughter, kindly agreed to come and play the other prostitute at very short notice when Naomi Campbell dropped out to promote her record.

37 [71]   Sera gets out of a car, spits on the street and lights a cigarette.

38 [65, 69]   Sera talks to her shrink (#4) about Ben, and how she was looking for him.

SERA

I don't know . . . it's just . . . I really like this guy. I mean . . . I've never felt anything for anyone that I've ever been with . . . as a trick . . . and it's . . . weird. I feel kind of confused about it. We were with each other for only one night but I felt like the relationship . . . you know . . . I felt like there was a relationship being formed and it was . . . I . . . I was kind of scared.

No . . . I don't think I should see him again. But I look for him. I went out last night and I was looking for him.

39 [74]   Ben and Sera meet on the street. She declines his offer of dinner.

I loved this location. In the background of the wide shot we see Bally's Casino, which has a constantly changing light show outside. We had no traffic control so the actors had to really push their voices to be heard. I am totally in favour of this. I hate it when the traffic is stopped and the voices get quiet and then in post-production the traffic is put back on again but somehow never sounds natural.

The ending was a Nic improv: 'We could get prime rib . . . they've got it on offer for $2.99 . . . I love that dress.'

I wrote a musical theme for *The Browning Version*. I'd negotiated a deal with Paramount and Ridley Scott (Producer), which gave me the right to compose the score. It became clear to me as soon as the editing started that this was not part of any master plan and at the earliest possible legal date I was replaced by Mark Isham. The same thing had happened on *Mr Jones* and a small picture I made with Juliette Binoche for HBO called *Mara*, based on a short story by Henry Miller. By the time *Leaving Las Vegas* came along I was more than a little insecure about my ability to compose. Annie Stewart suggested that maybe the *Browning* theme would work in *Leaving Las Vegas*. So, during the rehearsal week I played it to Nic and Lisa and also to Declan and Waldemar. Encouraged by their enthusiasm I included it in the ideas for the new score. It appears first in the motel room when Ben asks Sera to stay. It was used again here, as Ben says he wants to see her again. Part of the discarded *Mara* score also appears in the film.

40 [75]   Sera goes to a hotel to pay Yuri.
Without wanting to name-drop, Pedro Almodóvar says that this is his favourite scene because of the sound her skirt makes as she walks.

41 [76]   Yuri, paranoid at hearing voices through the wall mumbling in Russian, tells Sera he will never see her again. Tells her to leave.
Yuri's character was a real problem (and the result on film is a real credit to Sands) because he couldn't be too strong as he would then need to be paid off in a more dynamic way. Film language is very unforgiving. If you see a bad guy who uses violence then you expect to see him paid off with that violence. I had to avoid creating a scenario where the audience expects Yuri to jump out and be a threat to Ben's and Sera's love affair. This was not the nature of the story. On the other hand, he has to be strong enough to be believable as her pimp. I didn't want to show him being killed and I dropped the sequence where we see the gangsters' car driving into the desert with the body (Scene 82 in original). By bringing in Sting's version of 'My One and Only Love' as Yuri looks up at the gangsters at the door, we have already crossed over into the love story and never give him a second thought. The other thing I loved about Yuri's tale was that it reminded me of Hemingway's *The Killers*, which is one of my favourite American stories. I made him more philosophical than John O'Brien had and suggested to Julian that he accept his fate.

43 [*stolen from 75*]   Sera on the street looking for Ben.
I had no scripted shot here, but looking at the cut I realized that

we needed some air in the story otherwise we'd be in hotel rooms and restaurants for a long time. The shot was borrowed from the scene when Ben asks Sera to dinner.

44 [77]   Sera arrives at Ben's Motel and agrees to have dinner with him.

45 [80]   Over dinner Sera asks him why he is a drunk.

46 [79–8]   Ben and Sera on the street, walking. She asks him to stay with her.
The dialogue here was moved from the restaurant. I felt the developing love story needed as much time as possible. I notice though, that in other films couples fall in love within minutes (with a great deal of help from the score).

47 [78]   Sera's apartment. He tells her she 'looks extremely beautiful'.
These scenes were shuffled around because I wanted them to get on with their dialogue, get on with their relationship. After all, this is almost the halfway mark in the story.

48   Sera talks to her shrink (#5).

> SERA
> I mean . . . it's really weird because . . . um . . . you know, it's just like this thing's happening really quickly, you know . . . um . . . I just don't know what's going on. I mean . . . just the second I met him and the way I . . . I said my name . . . you know . . . I just said, hi, my name's Sera. And that's not what I do and . . . uhh . . . it's just it's all happening really quickly. I just felt like we were . . . we've been together for a long time. You know . . . it just felt so . . . easy . . . and . . . I felt like . . . um . . . I felt like . . . um . . . I felt like I was me. I didn't feel like I was . . . trying to be somebody else.

The therapy stuff was particularly useful here. Sera tells us she is in love.
It was strange for me. I've spent my whole life thus far being convinced of the power of the visual image over the spoken word. Now I realize how powerful a short sentence can be and how it can sometimes get to the point far quicker than a visual image.

Subtitles also have great power. The ending of *Montenegro* has an amazing subtitle.

The entire sequence from the end of scenes 42 to 48 is linked together by Sting's version of 'My One And Only Love'.

49 [*83*]   Ben wakes up in Sera's apartment. She suggests that he move in with her. He tells her that she can never ask him to stop drinking.

I can't remember any more if it was my intention, but many people have pointed out that when Ben asks her if she understands that she can never ask him to stop drinking, her answer, 'I do, I really do', sounds like a wedding vow.

50 [*84*]   Back at the motel Ben packs his case with booze. Talks to the camera.

51 [*86*]   Sera returns to her apartment to find Ben drunk at the gate with her landlady.

Laurie Metcalf kindly agreed to come and do a day's work. I first met her on *Internal Affairs* and agreed with John Malkovitch's remark that she is the finest actress around. She is amazing to watch. Any section of her work could be used to illustrate acting technique to students. Within minutes of Scene 51 starting she had everyone rolling in the aisles and I was very sad to see her go. I'd love to find a meaty role for her in the future. Meanwhile it's nice that *Roseanne* pays the bills.

51 [*87*]   Sera gives Ben two presents. They discuss the relationship. She suggests they go gambling.

John O'Brien's family turned up on the set while we were shooting this scene. It became difficult to continue working. I was aware of a wave of grief coming off them. I was also aware of how painful the experience must have been for them, given the autobiographical nature of the story. Much later they wrote to me and confirmed my suspicions, but added that in a strange way it had been a kind of a ceremony as well and had given them a sort of closure. His book has now gone into reprint and he is getting the kind of attention that I feel he deserves.

53 [*88*]   Ben and Sera walking on the streets.

54 [*89*]   In a casino Ben and Sera kiss.

We slowed this shot up and I used a little echo of the theme to play up the romance while still keeping it sad.

55 [89]   Ben has a violent fit in the casino and has to be restrained by security guards.
We shot two cameras nearly all the time and I operated the B camera. The shots leading up to the attack (where Ben is drunk but still cheerful), are running slightly slow because of a mistake that I made. We used my camera, an older Aaton, to film the underwater sequence (new Scene 66), and Declan thought it would be interesting to run at thirty frames per second instead of the usual twenty-four. We were so exhausted that the speed was not reset until we'd been shooting for quite a while the next day. However, we liked the results here; I think they accentuate the drunkenness. I like mistakes. At first I had no focus puller, there being not enough money in the budget. I did have a trailer, though, which I used twice a day to pee. I asked Marc Fischer whether I could trade my trailer for a focus puller and a day later Bonnie Blake turned up.

In the first draft, the scene in the casino was described by Sera to Ben in answer to his question the next morning: 'What happened?' After my conversation with Bill Tennent I decided to show the scene to illustrate the fact that drunks behave badly.

56 [90]   Ben wakes on Sera's sofa and has DT's. Tries to hold down some vodka and orange juice.
This scene evolved out of some research I did. I discovered that the stomach of an alcoholic contracts to about half of its normal size during the withdrawal state. As soon as any alcohol hits the stomach lining it relaxes to its normal size. The problem is that it is very difficult to hold alcohol in the stomach when it is contracted and so it is necessary to mix the orange juice with the vodka.

57 [91]   Ben gets into bed with Sera and he asks her to tell him about the previous night.
I would say that as much as anything the voice of Maggie Nicols was the key to the emotion of these last two scenes. She came into the recording studio and watched the section of film, listened to the underscore that I had already prepared and then went straight

into the booth and improvised. I think her work is outstanding. I first used her on *The House* (Channel 4, 1984).

58 [*92*]   Ben goes to buy some food but the store is closed.

59 [*93*]   Ben goes into a biker bar and gets into a fight. Gets head-butted.
Julian Lennon does a cameo here. We'd talked a few months earlier about his desire to get out of pop music and into drama, so I suggested he do a small role and see how he felt about the business afterwards. The day he came on the set the radio seemed to be playing John Lennon songs all day.

60 [*94*]   Ben meets the landlady on his way back to Sera.
The 'sexy, sexy' line is entirely Nic's.

61 [*94*]   Ben surprises Sera in the kitchen.
The only time on the film that Nic and I had a disagreement. I was a bit taken aback when he came in full of energy and strangeness and he misread my confusion for criticism. He did a subdued take, but it was not as good so we stayed with his interpretation. The quote 'Kling klang king of the rim ram room', Nic assures me, is from an early Sinatra song.

62 [*95*]   Ben and Sera in a mall. He is wearing new clothes. He goes down the escalator.
   The great thing about shopping malls in America is that they are all identical. This one is somewhere in LA and had huge cracks everywhere from the earthquake.

63 [*96*]   Ben gives Sera earrings. She says she will wear them at work. He reacts badly. He gets up to leave, but is persuaded not to by a stranger.
This cameo is by Bob Rafelson, director of one of my favourite films, *Five Easy Pieces*. I have known him for a few years and he has always been supportive and very entertaining with his stories of film-making. A very good man.
   The first mix of this scene had some emotional music on it, but I tried it without and realized that it wasn't necessary. I had some mall Muzak in the background instead

64 [*101*]   Sera leaves for work while Ben watches TV and drinks.

They agree to go on a short vacation together.

65 [106] At a desert motel they sit by the pool at night and watch *The Third Man* on TV.
Why *The Third Man*? It's one of my favourites but the real reason is a low-budget reason. I wanted them to watch a film. Lumière pictures sent me a list of all the films they own the rights to. This was one of them. I also loved the idea of that zither theme in the desert mixing with crickets and coyotes.

66 Next day by the pool. Ben goes underwater and Sera is concerned. She dives in and sees him drinking on the bottom of the pool. They kiss.

67 [108] Sera pours Scotch over her breasts and Ben kisses them. They get up to go inside, but Ben falls and cuts himself on a glass table.

68 [108] Sera attempts to clean up the glass. The desk clerk tells her to check out with Ben.

69 [110] Sera drives Ben back to Vegas.

70 Night-time shot of Vegas.
This whole sequence (Scenes 65–70) went through several versions both as script and then as edited footage. An earlier draft of the script had a scene on the way to the Desert Motel where Ben and Sera stopped the car and went for a swim in a lake. They both swam underwater but Ben was reluctant to swim up to the surface again and Sera had to persuade him. In pre-production we realized that this would be an expensive and time-consuming sequence so, reluctantly, I let it go from the script. When we were shooting in Vegas, Annie Stewart (Producer) told me that she'd spotted a perfect swimming pool for the scene. It was raised up above ground level and had windows on the side so that you could see the swimmers. I put it to the actors and they agreed to go for it. So, after a full night's shooting, on our way to the next location we stopped: just me, the actors, Declan and a few people to help us out. We were helped by the fact that Lisa is a brilliant athlete and could really control her movements underwater. We shot at thirty frames per second and, as I've already mentioned, later forgot to reset the camera. I saw *Casino* the other day and noticed

that Scorsese had used the same pool.

At the Desert Motel location I shot a scene where they come to the surface of the pool gasping for breath and Sera tells Ben that he'd frightened her. In the editing room I realized that it was redundant because we know what Ben's agenda is and don't need to be constantly reminded. The desk clerk (Susan Barnes) gives a chilling performance. I see this as the real turning point in the film. Any hope that Ben may be cured or saved has to be abandoned after this scene.

71 [*111–14*]   Ben wakes in the dark and goes to the fridge for vodka.
I had enough confidence in Declan to suggest going hand-held and shooting these three scenes in one. I'm very happy with the results.

72 [*115–16*]   Ben drinking vodka in the shower.
I did shoot the scene with him throwing up but it was very upsetting and almost unwatchable.

73   Ben and Sera sit down for food. Sera wants him to see a doctor.
At the end of this scene Ben uses his chopsticks to pick up a piece of ice. It struck me as the sort of thing that a drunk would do. It is the only time we see a solid pass his lips and the crunch of the ice as we fade to black is very strong. I can remember being immensely moved by Lisa's performance as we shot it. I looked around the set and could see that I was not alone in my opinion. It was interesting to see how she overcame everyone's preconceptions about her ability as an actress.

74 [*98, 100*]   Sera dresses for work.
Borrowed from an earlier sequence.

75 [*119–20*]   Ben at a casino table. Black-haired woman tries to pick him up.
The same woman who earlier observed Sera failing to pick up the conventioneer. I like trying to integrate the smaller characters as much as possible.

76   Flashback to photo burning, Sera kissing him, dice rolling. Electric billboard saying 'unfinished business'.

77 [*121*]   Sera comes home from work. Ben is with the other woman. Sera tells him to leave. She cries.

78 [*123, 125*]   Three college boys proposition Sera.

79   Dark, sinister shot of the glass pyramid.

80 [*127*]   Sera is raped by the boys in a motel.
A horrible scene to shoot for everyone involved. Lisa was fine until the physical stuff began, then she lost it. Every move was worked out with her before we shot and I decided beforehand that nudity was not necessary, neither was simulated sex.

81 [*129*]   Sera surveys herself in the motel mirror.

82   Sera hails a cab, standing next to huge fake waterfall.

83   Cabby is cynical with Sera.
Xander Berkeley has a great reputation among younger American film-makers. He worked with me on *Internal Affairs*. He came in for a couple of hours to do this role and clearly he wasn't concerned about appearing to be unsympathetic. A very good actor.

84 [*131*]   Landlady observes Sera limping home.

85 [*132*]   Sera bleeding in the shower has flashbacks to the rape.

86 [*133*]   Sera is evicted by the landlady and landlord.
David Brisbin (Landlord) is another actor who I know from Performance Art rather than cinema. He worked with Mabu Mimes and I met him doing a solo piece at the Mickery Theatre in Amsterdam which I filmed (*Rembrandt and Hitler or Me*). He also worked on *Mr Jones*.

87 [*138*]   Sera sits on the kerb as traffic goes by, drinking a coffee and smoking.
I changed this shot and I'm sorry that I did. In the first version, we see Ben in the background staggering past with a bag full of booze. Neither of them is aware of the other.

88 [*122*]   Slow-motion montage of Ben drinking and walking.
I like this effect – shooting straight into the sun but exposing for the shadow – and I used it in *Mr Jones*, but I think it got cut.

89 [*138*]   Back to Sera and traffic.

90 [*134*]   Sera goes looking for Ben at the 'Hole You're In' motel.

91   Sera on the streets looking for Ben. Blue night sky.
This was a comic moment in the Las Vegas shoot. A pair of
security guards came out to stop us filming. I tried to reason with
them, pointing out that the sidewalk (pavement in English) was
public domain. They disagreed and insisted that the casino owned
the sidewalk. Seeing that this was a no-win situation I asked them
if they felt that the casino owned the road in front of the sidewalk.
They thought long and hard about that one and then decided that
they probably didn't. My next question was whether it was okay
for Lisa to walk on 'their' sidewalk. They said it was okay for her,
but not the camera. So we put the camera in a car, opened the
window and kerb-crawled next to Lisa. I am learning. A gypsy
woman once told me that I should not confront situations but
swim around them like the Piscean that I am.

92 [*137*]   Sera in a casino is insulted by an Italian man in a white
suit.

93 [*140–41*]   Sera is evicted from the casino by security guard.

94 [*143*]   A sympathetic cab driver asks her what happened.
Lou Rawls is an actor as well as a singer and I jumped at the
chance to work with him. I also had the nerve to ask him to sing
'Stormy Monday' in the cab before he talked to Sera. However,
some months later, in the cutting room, it seemed very self
indulgent and I removed the singing.

95 [*142*]   Sera packs her bags and the phone rings twice. It is Ben.

96 [*145*]   Sera arrives at Ben's new motel. He is dying. They make
love.
This was the last scene that we shot and everyone began to dread
it. Nic lay on a bed of ice to get his body in spasm but it made a
lot of noise so he got rid of it. I think it probably helped to get him
ready, though.
    When I adapted the book I had a big problem with the ending.
In the book they do not make love; she masturbates him. This
would be very difficult to do in a film without alienating a lot of

the audience. The film was already a tough story. I kept it but then added the scene of her climbing on top and consummating their love. I expected a bad reaction to the masturbating, but so far it has not been even referred to.

97 [*145*] Sera sleeps and Ben wakes and then dies.

98 [*146*] Sera sits on the side of the bed next to Ben's body. Voice-over begins.

99 Sera in therapy (#6). Tells how she really loved Ben.

> SERA
>
> I think the thing is . . . we both realized that we didn't have that much time and . . . I accepted him for who he was. And I didn't expect him to change. And I think he felt that for me too. I liked his drama and he needed me. And I loved him. I really loved him.

100 Slow-motion clip of Ben which goes into freeze-frame. End titles. Sting sings 'My One and Only Love'.